To Jimmie an[d]
Cathe[rine]

on the happy occasion of the[ir]

golden wedding anniversary—

9 bless you—

Fr. T. Vinci SAC
Pastor

THE LIFE OF ST. VINCENT PALLOTTI

The Life of St. Vincent Pallotti

by John S. Gaynor, S.C.A.

ST. PAUL EDITIONS

IMPRIMI POTEST
Gulielmus Moehler, S.A.C.
  Rector Generalis

NIHIL OBSTAT
Nicolaus Ferraro, S.R.C. Adsessor
  Fidei Sub-Promotor G.ralis

IMPRIMATUR
+ Aloysius Cardinal Provicarius
  E Vicariatu Urbis

Grateful acknowledgment for this Authorized American Edition is made to the Irish Pallottines of Golders Green, 64 Armitage Road, London, N.W., England.

CONTENTS

Prologue

One day in the month of January of the year 1848, four men in the city of Rome engaged in a conversation on the current affairs of that city, which was filled with unrest. Pius IX had recently created a Council of State for the Papal States and was meditating a Constitution. Hardly anyone was pleased with the reforms he projected: the liberals because they were not liberal enough; the reactionaries because it meant opening the door to the demagogues and the dark forces which were swiftly taking up position behind them.

The four men were: Padre Gioacchino Ventura, an unnamed Monsignor of the Papal Court, a certain Signor Marchetti and the Anglican Archdeacon of Chichester, and over two of them the hand of destiny hung heavy. Father Ventura was a former General of the Theatine Order, the famous counter-Reformation society, which in its early days played a part almost as brilliant as its great contemporary, the Company of Jesus, in the religious affairs of those times. Ventura was famed throughout Italy as a preacher; he was, too, a voluminous writer on theological and philosophical subjects. His views were colored by the current Traditionalist philosophies and he was, at this time, a firm believer in a liberal solution for the problems of Italian society. He was a kindly generous man who sincerely supported the Constitutionalists without examining very carefully their characters or their motives. In the event he was to flee the country in disgust and in the year 1861, die in exile in Versailles, disillusioned and under a cloud. The Archdeacon of Chichester was Henry Edward Manning, a close friend of such great English Liberals as the Wilberforces and Gladstone, a steady member

11

of the Oxford Movement, a sound churchman, whose Romeward leanings were as yet not so pronounced as to alarm either himself or anyone else. Four years later he was to renounce Anglicanism and his liberal views, go on to be ordained a Catholic priest, found a religious community of men, become Archbishop of Westminster, play a commanding part in the Vatican Council, and finally die as a Cardinal of the Holy Roman Church. We have no information as to the subsequent career of the Signor Marchetti, and, of course, that of the Monsignor, whose name does not appear in our source, which is the Manning Diaries.

These men, all of them churchmen with the exception of Marchetti, sat and talked of the progress of the liberal policies and their chances of wholehearted acceptance by the important recalcitrants operating within the Catholic Church; the Archdeacon listened and took mental notes for his Diary. They were agreed, we gather, that a great obstacle stood in the way of the reforms: the Abbate Vincenzo Pallotti, whom they cataloged among the Obscurantists. His influence, it can be inferred from his talk, was not drawn from any political source, for he occupied no commanding position of power in the great city; in fact, no position at all, except the rectorship of an obscure little church, the headship of a little organization of ecclesiastics and of some charitable societies which he had founded. His influence came from the fact that he was regarded as a saint. "He sanctifies Obscurantism," said the un-named Monsignor. And the Padre Ventura complained that Pallotti had been seeing the Pope lately and had disturbed him by pointing out that the number of confessions and communions was dropping off alarmingly. By some convolution of inner logic, the Padre Ventura was able to persuade himself that this was a good thing, under the circumstances. "Now hypocrites declare themselves," he pointed out.

The Anglican Archdeacon had already heard about Pallotti from other sources. After his arrival in Rome, in November, he called on Newman, who was finishing his studies for the priesthood, and the great convert walked back with Manning to his lodgings. "Newman told me that there is a priest in Rome, named Pallotti, known for his sanctity, confessor to many of the chief people, Cardinals, etc., and that he had a sort of community." And a couple of weeks later, the Archdeacon's Roman mentor, a certain Broecchi, who was conducting an English-language newspaper in the city and often showed the sights to distinguished visitors, told him that "the Abbate Pallotti is a saint; a founder of regular clerks; he spends his life serving the sick and hearing confessions. He is the Pope's confessor." Manning is interested. On his way home one evening, he calls at Pallotti's church, takes note of the title of the Society, informs himself of the number of members, and notes, without comment, that there is a branch in London. And now at this meeting he hears Pallotti discussed from quite another angle.

The casual conversation of these men on that January day was nothing less than a restatement of a great and everlasting debate; whether goodness, or sanctity, if you will, should be employed as a means to an end rooted in human society, of whether its true issue is no other than religion and the Divinity. We know now that these men were utterly mistaken in their opinion that Pallotti was concerned with the politics of his day. There is no trace of *any* political opinion in his voluminous writings and correspondence. His only concern was religion, the Church, the means of grace and the union of men with God — sanctity. Because he achieved it himself and showed others how they too could do so, the Church has raised him to her altars: St. Vincent Pallotti, the nineteenth-century Apostle of Rome.

The life of a saint is worthy of examination, not only because of the influence he may have had on his contemporaries, but even more because he has succeeded in meeting successfully and heroically the greatest challenge with which man is faced: the subduing of his own nature, and, under God, his self-elevation into the high and serene regions where the Divinity peculiarly dwells. To give some idea of the factors involved, the means employed and the results achieved, is the purpose of this little book. And since Vincent Pallotti's path to sanctity is of the apostolic variety, his external achievements must also come into our story.

CHAPTER I

The Background

The particular branch of the Pallotti family
from which St. Vincent was descended can be traced
back to the middle of the sixteenth century and is
unremarkable. They were residents from that period
in the village of San Giorgio, which is a section of
the commune of Cascia in Umbria, the hilly country
made famous by the names of St. Francis of Assisi
and St. Rita. These Pallotti were farming folk, owning
their own land, which successive subdivisions
gradually reduced into uneconomic holdings. It
was part of a general process in the Italian countryside that the sons and daughters of the impoverished
farmers must emigrate, those of them who could, to
Rome and the other large centers of population, to
make another way of life for themselves and to send
back help to the relatives who stayed on the home-
stead.

Years after Vincent's death, when his name and
fame began to grow as a result of the proceedings
for his beatification, some of his biographers, following the example of some of the ancient hagiog-
raphers, timidly tried to establish that these Pallotti
were really a noble family come down in the world;
the assertion appeared to gain some credence when
Luigi Pallotti, Vincent's cousin, was made a Cardinal
and assumed a coat-of-arms. But there is no justification for the story. The Pallotti were people of the
soil.

The Umbrian peasants—and in particular the
peasants of Norcia—have always been skilled not only

in the tilling of their soil but in the preservation of food. We are, of course, writing about a period before the industrial age; there were no factories to absorb the emigrants to the cities, who were accordingly forced to seek their subsistence in the trades, if they possessed one, or in whatever occupation they could show some proficiency. The Umbrians appear to have found a way of life in the cities by trading in food. So it was with Peter Paul Pallotti, father of St. Vincent, who left his native village at the age of sixteen, in the company of a brother, in order to earn his living in Rome. In the division of the family property which took place before his departure, Peter Paul became the owner of a very small piece of land, less than an acre, which was left in the hands of his widowed mother. In Rome he found employment in a grocery, of which, in time, he became a partner, and later, the owner. He possessed business acumen for he eventually became the proprietor of several such shops.

In the year 1790, when he was thirty-three years of age, Peter Paul Pallotti was married in Rome to Maria Maddalena de Rossi, a young woman eight years his junior. She was herself a native of that city, where she was born on the little island, known as St. Bartholomew's which divides the waters of the Tiber in the vicinity of the broken arch of the bridge of Sublicius. Her family, whose circumstances were modest, had emigrated to Rome from the same region of Italy as her husband. An elder sister of Mary Maddalena de Rossi was a member of the Order of the Poor Clares, but the convent to which she was attached was suppressed during the troubles of the French Revolution and she found shelter, at first with the Pallotti family, and later in another convent of the Order which had been spared by the despoilers.

Peter Paul Pallotti and his wife rented an apartment in a building owned by the Teutonic College, in the picturesque, heavily-populated quarter of Rome, which surrounds the splendid palaces of the Chancellery of Holy Church. All their married life was spent in this house, which still exists much as it did then. Here Vincent Pallotti was born on April 21, 1795, and here he continued to live until his father's death in 1837. Sometime after his ordination to the priesthood he obtained permission to erect a private oratory in one of the rooms of the apartment, where he engaged in prayer and meditation and occasionally celebrated Mass.

Peter Paul Pallotti and Maria Maddalena de Rossi had ten children, five of whom died in infancy. The survivors were all boys, none of whom married, so that there are no lineal descendants now of Peter Paul Pallotti and Maria Maddalena de Rossi. Of the five who survived infancy, one died at the age of fifteen, another died in 1827, St. Vincent in 1850, and the other two survived him. With the exception of St. Vincent, none of them achieved particular distinction. One of them appears to have gone into business, trading in foodstuffs in a large way, but unsuccessfully, so that for the last years of his life he drew on his priest-brother, and later on his estate, to a considerable extent until his death; the other also relied largely on the family fortune. Peter Paul Pallotti must have realized the limitations of his children, for on his death he left all his property to Vincent, with the charge of providing as he thought best for his brothers.

Peter Paul Pallotti and his wife would be classified today as members of the small bourgeoisie; peasants turned shopkeepers, people of the lower middle class, that class which has so often been described as the backbone of western society. This particular couple were the parents of a saint, and it is therefore very relevant for us to inquire into their religious attitudes, as far as they can be ascertained. But before doing so, it is important to bear

in mind that the phenomenon of the growth of unbelief, as manifested among the Latin peoples of
the world, has for the past couple of centuries followed a fairly uniform pattern. The rejection of
Christianity as a theology and a way of life first shows
itself among these peoples in the upper classes of the
society: the aristocrats, the very wealthy, and the
intellectuals. In the course of a generation or two
the dry-rot spreads into the middle classes, the
professional people, the officials, the civil servants,
the teachers, the ordinary business people, the city
dwellers, and so on; and finally, in the third stage,
the peasantry and the working class are invaded.
(It may be an excessive generalization to say that the
re-Christianization proceeds in an inversely opposite direction, though there are considerable
evidences in favor of such a statement.) The notorious
irreligion of the French and Spanish ruling classes
previous to the outbreak of the French Revolution
had affected that same class in Italy at the same
period: here, too, the dissolvent acid of Jansenism
had been at work, and cultured scepticism was fairly
fashionable, but the people of the villages, the
countryside, and the small towns, were as yet free
from the corrosions of unbelief.

We have much evidence of the unquestioning
religious faith of Peter Paul Pallotti and his wife,
and of their great fidelity to the practices of their
religion. Some of this evidence is supplied by
St. Vincent himself, who wrote a touching memoir
of his mother, in which he describes the deeply
virtuous spirit in which she bore with the many
crosses of her lifetime and the saint-like manner
in which she prepared for death. Peter Paul Pallotti
was himself accustomed to hear at least one Mass
every day. These details, and many others, were
brought to light when Vincent's Cause came up
for examination in the diocesan court of Rome, and
the witnesses, who had known the couple, were still

alive to give testimony to what manner of people they were. From the same sources, we may gather information about the care with which they undertook the moral education of their children. "She took the greatest care (Vincent wrote in the Memoir mentioned above) to instruct us in the Christian Doctrine, to instill in us the fear of God and the horror of sin, doing all her own housework as long as she was able in order not to expose us to the possibility of bad example from servants. Not only did she shield us from temptation, but she also kept us busy in good works, in prayer, in study, in useful occupations...." The father, a busy merchant, was in the habit of hearing two or more Masses every Sunday and holiday, and it was his practice to take his children to church with him on such occasions.

The childhood of Vincent Pallotti does not, in any of the material details, reflect the troubled circumstances of the times. He went to school, he played with his companions among the grass-covered ruins, he took part in the boys' sodalities, attended the services in the various churches near his home. Meanwhile, during this very period, two Popes were arrested and carried off prisoners, within the span of ten years. The first of these, the aged Pius VI, died in exile, after a year's confinement in France. The Conclave in which his successor was elected had to be convoked in Venice instead of Rome, because the latter city was judged dangerous. The Pontiff who was on this occasion chosen, was, after some years, forcibly removed from the Papal Throne and taken to France, where he was held in prison for five years. The French armies, first the Republican, and then the Imperial, occupied the city of Rome on two occasions, and in their wake, governments inimical to the Holy See and to the deepest sentiments of the population were set up. In order to maintain themselves these governments sought and obtained the support of the worst element in the population. Secret societies sprang up and multiplied, some of them organized by patriotic, or merely adventurous men, for the purpose of getting rid of the foreigners; others were inspired by the usurping rulers for purposes of what today we would call counter-espionage. We all know that under such conditions both the jurisdictions—the civil and the ecclesiastical—suffer, parental authority is weakened, religion and morals become relaxed. Young Vincent Pallotti passed unscathed through it all, a favor which, under God, he owed to the solicitude and virtue of his parents.

Vincent's first letters were learned in a little neighborhood school, one of the many which the city authorities had always maintained in Rome. Here he spent a couple of years and then passed to the famous establishment conducted by the Fathers of the Pious Schools—the Order of St. Joseph of Calasanz—known as San Pantaleo, which is still in existence. Part of his secondary education was received here, and the rest at the Collegio Romano, the former Gregorian University, which, after the suppression of the Society of Jesus, had passed into the charge of a group of secular priests. His philosophical studies were commenced here and were concluded later at the Roman University.

The witnesses at the Process of Beatification and the early biographers have taken pains to point out that even in extreme youth Vincent Pallotti evinced an unusual interest in the details of religion. It was noticed that as a very small child he would gaze steadily and fixedly at an image of our Blessed Lady; as he grew older, he began to show much concern in the cultivation of virtue. He was, one gathers, a quiet, modest boy, who came and went, unobtrusively, through the crowded little streets which surrounded his home, but the sweetness of his manner, and the simplicity of his bearing attracted the attention of the neighbors and some of them recalled it very clearly fifty years later. They noted as well that he showed much compassion for the needs of the poor and that, so far as his circumstances allowed, he used to provide them with food and clothing, sometimes even giving away his own garments.

The development of Vincent's interior life is marked by a great milestone in the year 1807, when he was twelve years old. This was the year when he selected a certain Father Bernardino Fazzini for his confessor and spiritual director. The relationship lasted till Fazzini's death in 1837. One of the most important elements in every story of sanctity is the role played by the spiritual director of the elected soul. Let us therefore spend a little time setting down the main facts which are known about Fazzini.

He was a secular priest, who, at the time when Vincent selected him for his adviser, was the parish priest of a little church not far from the Pallotti home. When old age and infirmity made it impossible for him to do the outdoor duties of his parish, he resigned this office and became the chaplain of a hospice, where he continued, in spite of progressive blindness and paralysis of the limbs, to minister to the inmates. His death occurred in 1837, when he was over eighty years of age, and his spiritual son, Vincent Pallotti, assisted him during his last hours. Most of what is known about Fazzini derives from Vincent's references to him in his letters. We also learn something about him from the clear and unequivocal orientation, which, as is clear from the entries in Vincent's spiritual diary, Fazzini imprinted on the course of his interior life. Fazzini certainly played a decisive part in St. Vincent's entire life, even in the foundation of the Society of the Catholic Apostolate. This is corroborated by the fact that in the list which Vincent Pallotti drew up of the original associates, he placed the name of Fazzini in the first place of all, with his own name in the second place.

We gather that Fazzini's spiritual direction was founded on those traditional ascetical principles which stem right back to the Gospels. Thus he early introduced his spiritual child to the practice of corporal mortification, the discipline and other instruments of penance. The evidence goes to show that the spiritual director realized very soon that he was in the presence of a youth with unusual spiritual endowments, who desired very ardently to cooperate with the urgings of God's special graces, and Fazzini did not hesitate to lead him into the concrete paths of penance and mortification. Now, Vincent's parents and brothers got somehow to know of his secret corporal penances and his mother became alarmed, for her son was not very strong in health—he was, in fact, dogged by ill-health all his life, and several times was forced to take long periods of rest—so she decided to take up the matter with Fazzini, but the latter declined to make any changes in the method of his direction. He told her very simply: "the finger of God is here."

The little incident is interesting in a variety of ways. Vincent's relatives were thus given the assurance that the road he was beginning to tread was not just the result of his own choice, a mere youthful velleity, but was undertaken under responsible advice; if it was to be altered, it was the adviser who must alter it. That was what his mother went to ascertain at the fountain-head. The spiritual director, by using the phrase: "the finger of God is here," implies, very definitely, that the advice he has given his spiritual child is not based on ordinary considerations of spiritual therapy, but on the conviction that an extraordinary grace is being offered to this soul and it must be developed and cultivated by extraordinary means. And finally the incident is followed by the simple acceptance of them all: Vincent, the spiritual director, the relatives, that

God's ways of dealing with His creatures must not be opposed once it is clear that such is really His will.

It is very likely that even in his childhood, Vincent felt attracted by the priesthood. It is in the record that on one occasion, when he was a little boy, his mother was much surprised to find him playing ball on the street with other little boys; perhaps he was unusually boisterous, perhaps it was not his habit to play such games; anyhow she reproached him and his answer was: "Do not worry, Mother, you will yet see me saying Mass at the altar of St. Philip Neri." It is also known that in his case special care was taken regarding his education in Latin—the ecclesiastical language—as though the idea was already accepted in the family that Vincent was to be a priest. But vocations must not only be evoked; they must be cultivated as well, and this great task was performed by Bernardino Fazzini.

There came a moment in Vincent's spiritual development when the ideals and the austerities of the Capuchin Franciscan Order made a powerful appeal and he deliberated whether this was the road which God wished him to follow. He sought, of course, the advice of his director whose counsel was again decisive. It was given on two grounds, the first, that Vincent's vocation had to be fulfilled not in a monastery, but in the world; the second, that his health was not sufficiently robust to stand up to the rigors of a cloistered life. The decision was at once accepted, though Vincent retained all his life his affection and admiration for the great Capuchin Order. He even obtained permission to wear the Capuchin habit in his bed at night, a practice which he continued for many years, until a later spiritual adviser counseled him differently. One such habit is today treasured among the relics of his career which have been collected in the museum adjoining the room in the house where he died.

Vincent's final decision to enter the ranks of the secular priesthood was taken sometime in the year 1810, when he was fifteen years old. Let us now take a glance at the conditions under which candidates to the priesthood had to undergo their training at that particular period in history. The munificence of popes, prelates and princes had in past ages endowed the city of Rome with many splendid establishments for the training of aspirants to the priesthood. There were colleges, seminaries, and universities where the candidates of all conditions and nations might obtain all the advantages of the very best clerical education of the times. It was now the case, however, that the upheavals consequent on the French Revolution and the establishment of the French Empire had weighed heavily on these establishments all over Europe, and Rome was not an exception. The Roman seminaries and colleges were practically all closed and their revenues turned to other uses. Theology, philosophy and the sacred sciences continued to be taught at the Roman University, though this ancient establishment had been reorganized after the Napoleonic pattern common to all the Imperial universities. The church students were in reality deprived of all opportunity for community life of the kind on which the Church had been insisting since the Council of Trent for candidates to the priesthood. In consequence, these candidates were compelled, at the time when Vincent Pallotti made his studies, to live at home with their relatives and attend daily the lectures in the university. The supervision of their spiritual life and their fulfillment of the duties of their state devolved directly on the shoulders of the ecclesiastical authorities and the parochial clergy.

The matter of ecclesiastical garb at this period also had its peculiarities. The traditional vesture of the secular clergy from medieval times was the soutane, but during the seventeenth and eighteenth centuries, a modified version of this garment, the *habit court*, which consisted of a sort of frock-coat with knee-breeches and buckled shoes, came into use for street wear in the case of the secular clergy, not only in France, but also in Italy. The *habit court* of the clergy was easily distinguished from secular dress because of its black color. Religious, of course, always wore their habits in public and private. One of the effects of the French Revolution and the ensuing persecutions wherever that Revolution succeeded, was the abolition of the use of distinctive religious garb for public use. But when the end of the Revolution came and freedom was restored to the Church, a reaction in favor of the ancient style of dress for the clergy set in, particularly among the younger secular clergy, for whom the soutane became a symbol of their liberation from persecution. This tendency was supported by the ecclesiastical authorities, though in gradual fashion. Thus we find that the public use of the soutane was prescribed as obligatory for parish priests and rectors of churches in Rome by Leo XII in 1825. The unbeneficed clergy of Italy continued in some cases to employ the *habit court* for street wear for many years afterwards. Carlo Orlandi, for instance, who joined Vincent Pallotti's Society of the Catholic Apostolate in 1846 and was already a priest, was induced to change this vesture for the soutane, as he himself relates because of the silent example of Vincent Pallotti. There is evidence in the record to show that the movement in favor of soutane among the younger priests received much encouragement from Vincent Pallotti even before the publication of Leo XII's ordinance; previous to that period he himself had already begun to wear the cassock in public.

From what we have said above, the reader will readily apprehend why Vincent Pallotti spent all the years of his preparation for the priesthood under his father's roof, except for the periods of retreat each year and of preparation for the reception of Orders. During this time the influence of his spiritual director was, of course, paramount, and it is of interest for us to take note of the main characteristics which Bernardino Fazzini gradually brought to fruition in the elect soul which Divine Providence had entrusted to his care.

The first of these was his determination that Vincent Pallotti must mingle with his fellows and learn how to exercise leadership among them. There existed at this time a sodality whose object was to bring together the young candidates to the priesthood who were living in their homes in that part of Rome, for purposes of mutual encouragement and edification and for prayer in common. This sodality had its home in the chapel of Our Lady of the Tears — Santa Maria del Pianto — so called because it housed a famous image of Our Lady which, according to tradition, had shed copious tears when a young man hurried by in order to carry out a deed of vengeance sometime during the seventeenth century. Vincent Pallotti devoted his time and energies for many years to this sodality and in due course, it became his duty to instruct the junior members and aspirants, to arrange outings for them on holidays, to supervise their religious observances and community practices. Here he met Raphael Melia, who was later to become a priest, and the earliest member of all in the Society of the Catholic Apostolate, and was to work as a missionary in England for almost thirty years. This task in the sodality was absorbing and satisfying, as is attested by Vincent's correspondence which contains many details of his activities in this organization and those of the young men in his charge. It is indeed an unusual fact that so many of these letters, which are often concerned with day-to-day matters, were preserved at all; the explanation appears to lie in this, that the recipients realized even then, that these little documents emanated from an exceptional mind and heart. Fifty years later the holders surrendered them for the purposes of the Cause of Beatification.

This early conviction entertained by his disciples and clients that the memory of Vincent's words and works should be preserved was shared in fuller fashion by the mature mind of his spiritual director, who was quietly documenting Vincent's spiritual progress with material which his spiritual child was supplying him without any idea of the purpose behind the requests. It is very lamentable that Fazzini's papers were dispersed after his death and in consequence this important source of knowledge is denied us. Only one document from this collection has survived by some chance: the memoir of Vincent's mother written at Fazzini's request.

We do possess, however, Pallotti's spiritual diary, which he commenced to keep during the period of his preparation for the priesthood and continued till the end of his life. The Diary reflects his dialogue with his Creator and sets down the resolutions which, during retreats and other times, he formulated. More important still, it contains some account of the lights and graces which he received in prayer. It was written for no other eyes than his own, in simple heartfelt language, and it sheds the most vivid light on the course of his pathway to sanctity. The Diary commences in the year 1816, when he was twenty years of age, and concludes with the notes of the retreat he made six weeks before his death. The notebooks in which the Diary was written are three in number and are not continuous, inasmuch as sometimes he wrote in one, sometimes in another. The fundamental themes, however, run through them all like a golden thread, and when taken in conjunction with his published works and the various rules written for the instruction of his followers, it is not difficult to form a picture of the nature, the growth, and the maturity of his interior life. The Diary, we repeat, was not written for others; he regarded it as a statement made in the presence of God, expressive of what he wished to be and of how he longed to spend his life for the honor of God. On his deathbed, it is said, he asked for these notebooks to be placed near him, as though he wished them to continue to speak to God and to bear witness when his own heart and mind were to fail him at the end.

In the opening pages of his earliest Diary, he lays down for himself the principle that in all his actions, he will consult his spiritual director, and expresses the intention of constantly praying for him.

"It is my intention, now and always, to pray most fervently to God in Unity and Trinity, to our Lord, the most blessed Spouse of my soul, to Mary, my more than most beloved Mother, to the angels and saints and all the just, that God may grant, in the greatest abundance, light and grace to my director so that he may be enabled to lead me as quickly as possible by a road infinitely holy, secure, perfect and concealed from the eyes of men."

It became Vincent's practice to visit his spiritual director with great frequency, sometimes even daily. When he himself became the spiritual director of various colleges and religious establishments, he took the greatest care, sometimes at considerable expenditure of time and money, to be at hand as frequently as possible so that his spiritual children could have access to him whenever they wished. And when the time came for him to write a rule for the community of priests which he founded, the post of spiritual director in the community was endowed with unusual relevance. "The spiritual director," he says, "must be the soul of the house."

There is nothing spectacular in Vincent Pallotti's approach to sanctity, as manifested in his Spiritual Diary. The reference frame is that of the spiritual combat against sin and the struggle for virtue. Sin, repeated and unforgiven, leads to vice; vice leads finally to eternal destruction. Good actions, performed under the inspiration of grace and with a good intention, lead to virtue; virtue, multiplied and made permanent in the soul, leads to sanctity, which is union with God. It is one of the most ancient ascetic ideas in Christianity: the contrast between the light and the darkness, on which the old Fathers so loved to dwell and which we find already outlined in the Prologue of St. John's Gospel.

"In all my actions, prayers, teaching, study, and so on, I will endeavor (he writes) to imagine how these tasks would have been executed by our Blessed Lord, our Lady, the saints...and I will endeavor to confess my own shortcomings. Whenever I realize that I have failed in fulfilling these intentions, I will perform some act of the contrary virtue, with an act of sorrow for my shortcoming and I will endeavor to convince myself of my own wretchedness, using such words as these: 'The earth has given its fruits; I confess, O Lord, Your infinite perfection and the perfection of other beings and mine own great and almost infinite wretchedness and impiety.'

"And I will express my gratitude for each additional proof of my wretchedness and impiety...and I will note my faults down in writing so as to secure from my spiritual father whatever penance he may enjoin."

The existence of sin in the world and the weakness of human nature are facts just as patent as the existence of darkness. This is an admission which must be made and provided for at the beginning of the road towards perfection.

"I resolve (he writes in an early page of the Diary) for now and all time, and I wish to make this resolution from the depth of my spirit, never to consent to my own inclinations and to the incredibly great weakness of my most wretched nature...."

And when he came to write a rule for his followers, he lays down with solemn insistence that the first of all requisites for association with the community, a first requisite whose nature must be carefully explained and frequently repeated, not only to the neophytes but to all the members without exception, is "the spirit of sacrifice."

"The life of perfect and constant sacrifice among men consists (he writes in this rule) in the perfect, constant and universal practice of mortification of the disorderly passions."

The acquisition of this great virtue is to be made with the help of a great example: none other than the example of our Lord in the Incarnation, the Circumcision and the other mysteries of His life on earth; an example, however, with a difference, for as Pallotti is careful to point out, it is "among men" that mortification of the disorderly passions is an essential requisite, for in the case of our Lord, none such existed. The timeless ascetical principle which lays down, that temptation, sin and vice are to be combated among men by the cultivation of the virtues which bear against them, and in particular by the virtues as apprehended through the meditation and imitation of the life of our Lord, is a cardinal principle in the spiritual life of Pallotti and of all those who would tread his way. Deceitfulness, for instance, is to be kept at bay and destroyed by truthfulness; lust by purity; pride by humility.

Parallel to this resolute struggle for virtue and sanctity, the early pages of the Diary reveal the presence of a vehement aspiration in his will; an unlimited desire to contribute in every possible way to the infinite glorification of God. This twenty-year-old youth, who quietly walked the streets of Rome to and from his university classes every day, who gave up his spare hours to the little tasks of leadership in the Sodality, who awaited every morning the opening of the door of the neighboring church in order to make his morning prayer before the Blessed Sacrament and to hear the daily Mass, who was modest, kind and helpful to the poor, simple and sparing in his speech, who betrayed no ambition of any kind, but went unobtrusively about his allotted occupations—this young man was consumed within by the flame of a most profound realization of the glory and majesty of God's infinity and of man's duty to glorify Him, beyond all the possible limitations of time and place.

It is not, of course, a singular attitude; other saints and mystics in the long history of the Church have demonstrated similar preoccupations, but no reader can fail to be struck by the ardor with which young Vincent Pallotti embraced this ideal, the constancy with which he followed it all his life, and the extraordinary force of the language which he employed in order to express it. It was, without doubt, a mystic grace. We may, however, essay an interpretation which supplies a reason why it was vouchsafed just at this period of his spiritual development, and why he employed so very special and striking a terminology in his endeavors to correspond with it.

He was at this time engaged in the study of the early part of his theological course. Following the usual practice of the period, the students, in addition to availing themselves of the textbooks recommended by each professor for his subject, were in the habit of taking copious notes in class: notes which were later transcribed in a fair copy which then became a substantial element for the preparation for examinations. Vincent Pallotti's notebooks for his philosophical and theological course were carefully preserved and hence it is possible for us today to determine not only what books and texts he used, but also the special emphasis which each professor laid on each subject and to some extent even the special profit which the compiler of the notebook could derive from such treatment. Among these treatises one is

struck by the quality of the lectures of the great
Tractate on the divine unity and the discussion
of the attributes of God, in particular His infinity.
No one, who either in private study, or in a theological class, has learned the significance of these great
doctrines and has sensed something of their profun-
dity, can fail to understand how contemplation is
nourished and action is stimulated when these
mighty verities really become the possession of the
mind which addresses itself to them.

God is the Alpha and the Omega; the true end
of man is the glory of God. He alone is the Absolute,
all other beings are relative to Him; all beings praise
God according to their natures; being transcends
time and space and actuality — when great conceptions
such as these are taken out of the range of mere
intellectual assent and are mysteriously urged by
grace and converted into sources of action: in such
a context, statements like this in Vincent Pallotti's
Diary become intelligible and lead us on to wonder
and veneration:

"It is my intention that whatever good deeds have
been done, are being, or will be done, by all beings, as
well as what I myself have done, am doing, or will do,
for the supreme glory of our God and heavenly Father,
most beloved and infinitely perfect — that these deeds
should be done with infinite perfection, insofar as this is
possible. And not only in the case of beings who have so
acted, but also in the case of all existing and possible
beings, rational and irrational, sensitive and non-sensitive."

The contribution thus offered to God's infinite
glory, even after the exclusion of all the temporal
limitations, did not still satisfy his interior longing,
which he went on to project into another dimension:

"I will imagine to myself that all these beings have
existed from all eternity and will continue to exist for
all eternity, and that each one of them is infinitely multiplied each infinitesimal moment, and these moments,

themselves multiplied into infinity: that each being is infinitely multiplied each moment for all eternity; that each molecule of every body is infinitely multiplied in every infinitesimal moment of time from all eternity to all eternity...."

This statement of his vision of the progression of beings into near-infinity is not a mere intellectual exercise, a philosophical play upon words; he goes on to dwell on the perfection which he desires that these beings, each in his order, should possess in virtue of the fact that they are creatures of God, whether actual or possible.

"It is the desire of my soul that each of these beings should possess the perfections of all creatures, infinitely multiplied...that they should possess infinite faith, hope, charity, contrition, prudence, justice, temperance, fortitude, humility, mortification...."

His purpose in enumerating all these splendors is quite simple. He does so in order to offer them all to the infinite glorification of God. And then he is led to contrast his own human condition with the greatness of the offering he wishes to make.

"Invoking now the assistance of the most high God, infinite, immense, limitless, and pleading for the mercy of the Lamb of the living God and imploring the protection of my Lady and our common Mother Mary, and of the angels and saints, I will reflect on my own misery, which is very great, not to say infinite, and realizing, that it is absolutely impossible for me to do all this, because of my wretchedness, blindness, ignorance, volubility, inconstancy and impiety in the highest degree, from the depths of my own nothingness, I will cry out from the bottom of my heart: 'Lord, O Lord, I confess in the presence of Your infinite perfection and that of Jesus and Mary and of the angels and saints and of all other beings, that my misery, poverty, blindness, ignorance and impiety are very great and infinite....'"

In spite of these shortcomings and imperfections, whose magnitude appears to him all the greater by reason of the contrast with the excellence of the offerings made by other creatures of God, his mind remains fixed on one thing: "I vehemently desire that great glory, even infinite, be given to my celestial Father, and since I acknowledge that I am unable to give it, I will humiliate myself in spirit."

For the convenience of prayer, he declares that the explicit enumeration of all the aspects of his desire to glorify God in all His creatures is concentrated in the use of the word: *Domine,* though from time to time, he resolves to make the enumeration in full; he attaches also a special significance to the repetition of the same word, in the phrase: *Domine, Domine.*

Vincent's ardent desire to glorify God in His infinity is a sentiment as real and true as his conviction of sin and his desire for sorrow. He therefore formulates the intention of projecting this conviction and this sorrow, as far as man's finiteness allows, into the same limitless region where his mind ranges, in order to give God all the glory which is His due:

"It is my intention to ask pardon of God for my sins at every moment, infinitely multiplied from all eternity to all eternity, burdened with all the sorrow of all beings, and those of Jesus and Mary: imagining myself to be prostrated face downwards on the road to Damascus with St. Paul, and asking pardon, together with him, and with St. Peter, and with the Good Thief on the cross, and with Mary Magdalene...."

The things of this world, whether visible or invisible, also serve God; human beings can use them in their search for the Divinity. There comes however a moment in the ascent of the soul to God, when all such objects must be purged of their material significance and be henceforth seen and used, as it were, through God's eyes. At some moment before he was ordained priest, Vincent Pallotti endeavored to look in this way on all the goods of this world. He penned the following lines in his Diary:

"Not the intellect, but God.
Not the will, but God. Not the soul, but God.
Not hearing, but God. Not smell, but God.
Not taste and speech, but God.
Not breath, but God. Not touch, but God.
Not the heart, but God. Not the body, but God.
Not the air, but God. Not food and drink, but God.
Not clothing, but God. Not rest, but God.
Not the goods of the world, but God.
Not riches, but God. Not honors, but God.
Not distinction, but God. Not dignities, but God.
Not advancement, but God. God always and in everything."

Thus, following the inspiration of divine grace and the guidance of his spiritual director, Vincent Pallotti ascended the traditional steps which lead to sanctity: the mortification of the flesh, the effort to know, serve, and glorify God in His uniqueness, the recognition of and repentance for sin, the correct evaluation of the things of this world, the complete acceptance of God as the only true and final reality — "God always and in everything."

In the presence of this extraordinary and most vivid consciousness of the infinity of God, as it appears in the extracts we have given above, which have been chosen almost at random, the reader may well ask whether Vincent Pallotti reserved this form of prayer to himself, or did he endeavor to hand it on to those whom in later life he strove to form in sanctity? The answer is that when the time came for him to found his institute, he gave it for its motto, the words: "For the infinite glory of God." In the common prayers which he laid down for the communities of his rule, his famous "intention" appears again and again; it is to be found as well in the prayers which he drew up for the external associates of the community. The institute itself was entitled "The Society of the *Catholic* Apostolate" with the stress laid on its universality; and he refused to include in the rule, such obligations and ties as might tend to limit the universality of its scope. Its purpose, as we shall see, was to serve the whole Church, and the entire cause of religion, without any restrictions whatever. There were no frontiers in his prayer and he placed no frontiers on the apostolate which he wished his followers to practice.

There is another substantive element in his religious life which we will mention now, for it appears in the earliest pages of his Diaries: his understanding of and his compassion for the poor and the heavy-laden, whom he wished with all his heart to succor.

"I think about and see and hear of so many afflicted persons, in anguish and travail, worn out, burdened and occupied by their labor and their heavy burdens, such as the poor tradesmen, peasants, carriers, carpenters, bricklayers, the poor women afflicted with their domestic cares, anguished, in ill-health by reason of sleepless nights occasioned by the illnesses of their children, whom they must look after and care for. I am impelled to reflect on the great afflictions which weigh down so many poor families, discords among husbands and wives, disputes among brothers and sisters and among relatives and friends, the oppressions to which so many young women are exposed, the poor estate of fatherless children and unprotected widows, the neglect, contempt and suffering of the poor of Christ, the sufferings of poor slaves, and those in prison. And there are so many other miseries which I have not enumerated because I am not even aware of them! All these things afflict our poor common nature in such fashion that if I or anyone else were to gather all these things into one point and look on them, I believe most firmly that the human heart would not bear such a sight, but would die of sorrow. I shall, in consequence, excite within myself a lively compassion for all these creatures of God and succor them in accordance with the rule of Christian charity and holy prudence."

"He helped the poor." Many years ago this writer, while doing his studies in Rome, met an old man, who at that time was over ninety years of age and remembered in his extreme youth being taken to the funeral of Vincent Pallotti. When asked what he knew about Pallotti, his answer reflected the only conscious memory which survived in him; it was to this effect, that "Pallotti helped the poor." Here we are referring, of course, to Vincent's general attitude towards the victims of poverty, for we shall have occasion later on to see which were the concrete measures he took during his lifetime to alleviate human misery.

Vincent's overmastering desire to "intend" and to do everything for the infinite glorification of God led him on with inexorable logic to commit himself to the apostolic forms of life of a priest working actively among his fellowmen. The necessity and urgency of promoting God's glorification among His creatures is the ultimate purpose of every apostolate. In the portion of his Diary which was written while he was still an ecclesiastical student, we find the following considerations:

"There are many sinners, heretics, and infidels, many souls which if they were properly directed, would perform great deeds in the pathway of the Lord; many unlearned people, who if they were instructed, would be great saints; many learned people, who, if they were only a little less learned, would be more humble and saintly; a very large multitude of people who suffer from spiritual infirmity.... I shall endeavor to excite in myself a great desire to instruct, enlighten, regulate, sanctify, perfect and convert all these souls with infinite perfection (were this possible) on my part and theirs, for God's infinitely great glory...."

When, therefore, Vincent Pallotti founded his Society of the Catholic Apostolate "For the infinite glory of God," he was planning that his collaborators and followers should proceed along the same path which he had trodden. The worship of God's infinity leads on to the total commitment of the whole man to the Divinity. And every man who has selected this ideal must strive, in apostolic fashion, to bring all other men to the knowledge and love of God. As Pallotti repeated again and again, it was necessary to "rekindle faith and charity throughout the world."

CHAPTER II

First Steps in the Priestly Apostolate

Vincent Pallotti's ordination to the priesthood took place on May 16 of the year 1818, three weeks after his 23rd birthday. According to the custom of the time, he had been ordained to the sub-diaconate and the diaconate, eighteen months and one year respectively, previous to this date. The notes of his retreats in preparation for these Orders are extant in his Diary and from them it is apparent that his mind was deeply concerned with the change of *state* which the reception of Holy Orders implies. The outward and external observances of the cleric in Holy Orders, the gravity and decorum which he must observe, the nature of the duties which he must now perform when ministering at the altar and reciting the breviary, are all reviewed in his notes. But beyond and above these observances, he is concerned still more deeply with the obligation of interior sanctity which the Orders carry with them. Previous to their reception he had, with the consent of his spiritual director, made private vows of chastity, of poverty, in accordance with the guidance to be supplied by his director, and also of obedience to his director. To these he added a fourth vow, that of maintaining the doctrine of the Immaculate Conception, which at this period was not yet a defined dogma of the Catholic Church.

Shortly after his reception of the sub-diaconate, he resolved to take advantage of the discipline and the spiritual privileges of the Secular Third Orders, and he therefore joined four such associations; the

Tertiaries of the Minims of St. Francis de Paola, the Carmelite, Franciscan and Dominican Tertiaries, and after the usual interval he made his profession in these organizations, shortly before his ordination to the priesthood.

At the period of history when Vincent Pallotti received Major Orders, the practice of being ordained "on the Title of Patrimony" was still frequent. For those who may not be acquainted with the significance of this term, it may be useful to observe that the Catholic Church demands, before conferring Major Orders, that the candidate, who in his new state will not be permitted to pursue secular avocations, shall show that reasonable means of support for him are at hand. In the case of secular priests this may consist of the certification of the bishop of a diocese that he will undertake this obligation (the Title of Service of the Diocese): it may also consist of the settlement of a certain patrimony on the candidate by his relatives (the Title of Patrimony). All clerics must, of course, be subject to their bishops, but a greater latitude was allowed in declining, or accepting, ecclesiastical offices in the case of those ordained on patrimony; they were not obliged, except under unusual circumstances, to become curates or parish priests. Vincent Pallotti was ordained on the Title of Patrimony.

The ceremony of his ordination to the priesthood took place in the Cathedral of St. John Lateran, and on the following day, which was Trinity Sunday, he celebrated his first Mass in a little church in the town of Frascati, the well-known hillside resort a few miles from Rome. Here his family had the use of a villa where it was their custom to spend some time during the summer months. It may be surmised that their convenience was consulted when Vincent chose this place for his first Mass. He was familiar with the neighborhood, for he used to accompany his relatives here during the holiday period and it was his practice at such times to employ himself in the teaching of catechism to the children of the peasants. It' was, in fact, in Frascati, where he preached his first sermon, while still in minor orders (in accordance with a custom which existed in Italy at that time). This was two and a half years previous to his priestly ordination.

Two months after this event, he rendered his final examination at the Roman University and was awarded the degree of Doctor in Theology and Philosophy. The examination results of Vincent's entire academic career are extant and they show that while not of unsurpassed brilliance, no examination was ever repeated, and on several occasions he was awarded prizes. At the end of his philosophy course, he was classified "among the first" and in the classical language department, he was awarded the title of professor of Greek. The title of professor of philosophy and arts was also conferred upon him during the course of his studies. In the final examination of his career, the result was judged so satisfactory, that an unusual reward was granted to him. This was a small pension, thirty crowns yearly, which the university awarded to those students whose performance was considered so far above the average as to merit it.

His possibilities as a teacher were readily put into service by the university authorities, for early in 1819, a few months after he received his degree, he was appointed a member of the Academy of the university and was placed in charge of the theological seminar. This institution was frequented by the advanced students who wished to perfect themselves in the orderly exposition of theological theses. Attendance was in the beginning voluntary but in view of the success under Vincent's direction it was made obligatory for all students who were aspiring to receive degrees. His duty entailed daily attendance at the university, the selection of the subjects to be debated, the designation of the persons who were to intervene in the argument, and the supervision of the debate itself.

His pupils, as was later testified, noticed several things about him. In the first place, in that age of ceremoniousness, the young academician, who was entitled to wear the doctoral biretta on such occasions, never did so. There was a rostrum in the hall where the disputations were held and it would not have been unusual if he presided from it, in state, but it was his habit to mingle with the students and participants, without assuming an air of precedence over them. And finally, they perceived that he was thoroughly conversant with the substance of the matters dealt with, and that, above all, in an age when the name of St. Thomas Aquinas was not held in the same esteem as it has been for over a century since, down to our own times, he seemed very conversant with the views of the Angelic Doctor on matters theological.

For ten years, he held this academic post. Among his pupils there were many young men later destined to make their name in posts of responsibility in the Church — at least three future bishops and four future Cardinals. As time went on, however, it became clear to Vincent that this work, however congenial because it gave him an opportunity to exercise an apostolate among his brethren of the clergy — which was always an object dear to his heart — did not satisfy fully his special vocation. Gradually other tasks and undertakings were placed in his hands and the conviction came upon him that it was his duty to utilize all his time and energies in the manner which Providence was unfolding to him. Finally, after ten years of service in the Academy, he resigned in order to be free to dedicate himself more completely to other forms of the apostolate among the laity and the clergy. His work for the clergy did, in fact, increase as the time passed, for he was appointed spiritual director of several important seminaries and colleges.

The academic aspect of his apostolate for the clergy did not, however, come to an end with his resignation, for he later established, with great success, a weekly conference for ecclesiastics, which had a large attendance and continued to perform a valuable work among the Roman clergy for many years after Vincent's death.

What was the population of Rome like, in the third decade of the nineteenth century, when Vincent Pallotti first addressed himself to the problem of how to "revive faith and rekindle charity," to use his favorite formula, among the people of his native city? One of Italy's greatest philosophers, the gentle and saintly Antonio Rosmini-Serbati, the founder of the great Institute of Charity, was in Rome in 1829, on the business of his foundation, and he has left us this description of the contemporary scene:

"For the person of moral sensibilities, this is an undefinable city; all the elements are mingled together; everything is present and nothing is bothered about; the people, in appearance at least, are sunk in profound apathy. They live in a state of astonishment at what happens to them and at what is going on around them; there is much ignorance and much admirable good sense; superstitious opinions are heard on all sides and at the same time there is the most sensitive discernment in religious matters; there is popular laxity and popular rigorism; one may hear on the lips of the people, the most profound judgments on all topics and at the same time everything is treated with levity and jocosity. Present-day Catos are to be found in the Trastevere. The government is the most paternal and beneficent existing in the world. Attachment to it is limitless and is not capriciously expressed, because that attachment has become habitual and forms part, as it were, of the very nature of the Romans."

Surveying the same scene from a distance of 150 years and viewed in the light of the direful experiences of our own generation, one gets the impression from this writer and others of the period that the people of Rome lived in a society almost without cadres; masses of people whose institutions were approaching exhaustion; energies being poured into individual action, to the neglect of organization and social cohesion. How right Vincent Pallotti was in formulating his plan of Catholic organization, namely the Society of the Catholic Apostolate, which was the forerunner of modern Catholic Action!

These were not, however, a population of simple and ingenuous individualists. Here is another judgment on the inhabitants of Rome, made by one of the most acute Italian social observers and public men of our time, Egilberto Martire:

"The contemptuous harshness of this people — which finds expression even in the rhythm of their dialect — is not a manifestation of simplicity. There is nothing of the candor of the primitive about them, not even in their illiteracy. The experience and the wisdom of twenty-seven centuries of civilized life lies behind everything, even their vices and their virtues. Even their most deplorable vituperations, their facility for criticism, their tendency to satire and litigiousness, are but the reverse picture of a people inured to greatness, to the command of themselves and of others; a people ready to despise danger and put up with suffering. One observes moreover the felicitous conjunction of a taste for irony and an appreciation of the relativity of human existence, which leads on to indulgence and tolerance and preserves them from the dangers of intransigence and despotism; which prevents the moral sense from degenerating into puritanism and saves religion from falling into superstition and bigotry...."

Such were the people among whom Vincent Pallotti, the mystic with his whole mind and will intent on the glorification of God, the penitent profoundly penetrated by the sense of human unworthiness and sin, was to expend the energies of his priestly life. He was one of them, in all senses of the word, for his roots were in the masses and not in the aristocracy nor in the administrative classes of society.

We have mentioned above the Pallottian apostolic ideal: "the revival of faith and charity." Every sensitively religious person at this period realized that some change was operating in the deep sources of Italian society, whose results were manifesting themselves in an increasing hostility towards the supernatural principles of religion. The gentle Pius VII, he who was to suffer so much in his own person, realized this even before the worst of the storm burst upon him. He wrote, as follows, in July, 1806, to his Nuncio in Paris:

"We are in God's hands, who knows whether the persecution which threatens us has not been decided by the decrees of heaven in order to bring about the revival of faith and to reawaken religion in the hearts of Christians."

The reader will notice that the Pallottian formula "revival of Faith" is employed even at this stage by the harassed Pontiff.

Pius VII returned to Rome from his long imprisonment in France shortly before the fall of Napoleon; the Congress of Vienna in 1815 restored to the Church the ancient Patrimony of St. Peter. The necessity and the urgency of a general reform, not only in the civil administration of the papal states and in the details of management of church affairs, but also in the whole attitude of the Church towards the new generation, was widely advocated. The word "reform" was in the air. Consider the magnitude of the problem, as stated by Cardinal Wiseman in his well-known work "Recollections of the Four Last Popes."

"The Church and the State (he is writing about the period after the return of Pius VII to Rome) had almost to be reorganized, after such devastation as had almost completely swept away the ancient landmarks. New kingdoms had arisen which literally effaced the outlines of old ecclesiastical jurisdictions, and even what before had been a Catholic state had come under Protestant domination. Conventual life and property had been annihilated in most of Europe; canon law had been abolished, church endowments had been confiscated; civil codes had been introduced at variance with ecclesiastical jurisprudence; the authority of bishops had been deprived of all means of enforcing their decrees: in fine, a state of things had been produced totally different from what the Catholic world had ever before seen."

These things, however deplorable in themselves, could be rectified in time by wise laws, able administrators and skillful diplomacy. Even the economic and financial disasters and depredations could be mended by clever men, but the very people had changed; new laws, administrative reforms, structural modifications where called for, but of themselves they would not prove sufficient. It was necessary to get at the hearts of the people.

The administrative reform, which was commenced in the latter years of the pontificate of Pius VII, reached its high point in the reign of the succeeding Pope Leo XII. The finances of the state were placed under rigid administration, some taxes were abolished altogether, others which weighed unfairly on certain classes of the population, were redistributed more equitably, a new code for the administration was published; education in all its branches, primary, secondary and university, was reorganized; the hospitals, the prisons, the police force were reformed; the charitable societies were reconstituted under new bases; the entire parish system of Rome was reviewed and readjusted; laws dealing with the endemic evil of brigandage were enacted; measures were taken against the secret societies; the retail trade in wine, which had led to widespread intemperance and habits of violence among the population, was curbed; the seminaries and ecclesiastical institutions of learning reopened; the practice of popular missions was powerfully encouraged.

All excellent measures, each in its own degree, but a change of heart among humans can only be made by penetrating into these hearts. The contact of person with person must be established and the giver must have some real gift to impart to the receiver. This was the role which God's Providence had reserved for Vincent Pallotti and the other holy people who lived in Rome during the first half of the nineteenth century — St. Gaspar del Bufalo, Blessed Anna Maria Taigi and others, who in the course of our story will appear.

St. Gaspar del Bufalo, founder of the Congregation of the Most Precious Blood, occupies with Pallotti a primary place in the apostolic efforts of this time. Ordained priest in 1808, he declined to take the oath which the Imperial Government imposed at that time against the rights of the Holy See in the Papal States and had to flee the country. On his return to Rome after the fall of Napoleon he was immediately appointed Adminstrator of the Hospice of Santa Galla in the city of Rome. This Hospice was in its day one of the most remarkable organizations in Europe. Founded by the Odescalchi family in the seventeenth century, the charter was a model of its kind. Its purpose was to provide lodging and assistance, both material and spiritual, for the large numbers of migrants who, from ancient times, were wont to come to the city, in search of work or driven from their own homes by some calamity. It offered hospitality to the troops of carters, vendors of wine, fruit, hay and other produce, whose occupations obliged them to spend some days in Rome between their trips. The victims of misfortune and the simple traders needed protection from the gangs of adventurers, exploiters and other criminal types who would have battened on them unless the Hospice of Santa Galla stood between them and their victims. Food, lodging, medical help, legal assistance, religious instructions and other forms of true social service, were provided for them by the great Hospice.

The religious instruction in Santa Galla was given by a Pious Union—that is, a religious sodality whose members, without prejudice to their state of life and other religious obligations, undertook to perform certain tasks under the direction of the superiors of the union. These were assisted by a council of priests, chosen for their apostolic spirit; it was generally considered a high, if arduous honor, to belong to this council. In 1815, the head of the entire organization was Monsignor, later Cardinal, Charles Odescalchi, whose name will appear again.

In the year 1815, Vincent Pallotti, who had just commenced his theological course and was being encouraged to do active apostolic work by his spiritual director, applied to the Pious Union of Santa Galla in order to share in the teaching of catechism to the Hospice dwellers. He was admitted to membership and thus began his long friendship with St. Gaspar del Bufalo, which ended in this world at St. Gaspar's deathbed, beside which Vincent knelt and prayed when the last summons came.

In the letter communicating his admittance to the Pious Union dated December 4, 1815, Vincent Pallotti was requested to take charge of peasants sojourning in Rome. From a note written by him on the back of the letter, we learn that he determined, after consultation with his spiritual director, to gather them together on the eves of feasts, in order to give them religious instruction. The group with which he was specially entrusted consisted of the vendors of hay. These had their stance on what was then known as the "campo vaccino"—the great grass-grown open space between the Capitol and the Church of St. Frances of Rome—an expanse dotted with out-crops of rubble and ancient masonry.

The open space is still there, but it is no longer covered with grass, for it has been excavated and is known today all over the world as the Roman Forum. Old prints of the period sometimes depict the great wains of the hay-sellers, with their trains of oxen and the attendant peasants standing around garbed in the attire of their native villages. These people, excepting the usual guards, would normally seek their rest in Santa Galla, which stood nearby.

Vincent Pallotti composed a manual of rules governing the spiritual assistance which he was to render these people. Though it is not explicitly stated in the manual, it is certain that he brought in several people to assist him in the work which consisted in gathering the hay-vendors together in a large room and there instructing them in the truths of the Christian religion and leading them on to the reception of the sacraments. The instructions, he points out, are to be illustrated with examples and instances taken from the lives of the saints. These hay-vendors had some form of organization among themselves, for Vincent established in his rules that previous to the meetings, it was well to make arrangements privately with the leaders of the groups, in order to secure as large an attendance as possible.

The relationship of Vincent Pallotti with St. Gaspar del Bufalo at this period, when Vincent was not yet even ordained, was further strengthened by the fact that St. Gaspar was at the same time the Secretary of the Confraternity of Christian Doctrine in Rome; a venerable organization which had been founded centuries before by Cardinal Baronius. Among the Pallotti papers there are several rules for the management of catechetical unions among youths of both sexes and as well as for the imparting of religious instruction in schools; these rules were drawn up as a result of the collaboration of the two saints; one, an experienced laborer in the vineyard of the Lord: the other, a beginner in the wide field of the apostolate.

St. Gaspar was a great popular missionary, much of whose time was given to delivering missions in the towns and cities of Italy, and there came a moment when Vincent felt that perhaps he should give himself completely to this type of work, but his spiritual adviser remained firm in his judgment that Vincent had a special vocation, which had to be fulfilled in a special way.

The congregation founded by St. Gaspar is dedicated, as its title shows, to the diffusion of the devotion to the Most Precious Blood among the faithful. Vincent shared in this enthusiasm, became a member of the Pious Union which St. Gaspar founded and urged his friends and penitents to join it. Later on, when the Society for the Catholic Apostolate was founded, St. Gaspar reciprocated by becoming a member of the Pious Society erected by Vincent.

There was a certain Canon Mucciolo who had established a society for boys of the poorer classes, a sort of academy where they were instructed in useful knowledge and in the doctrines of religion. The boys had their meeting-place in a building alongside the Tiber, just at the point where the famous broken arch of the Bridge of Sublicus divides the course of the river. The canon's enterprise therefore became known as the Work of Ponterotto—the Broken Bridge. There came a moment when the Canon felt that he needed help in his task, so he approached Vincent Pallotti, who, from the year 1820 onwards, became associated with Mucciolo in this enterprise. A time further arrived when Mucciolo decided to put Vincent at the head of the entire undertaking, but he could not be prevailed upon to accept. Finally, the ecclesiastical authority intervened and Vincent became the Vice-Rector of the work of Ponterotto. His work here embraced the teaching of the catechism, the delivery of lectures and the periodical preaching of retreats in preparation for the general Communions of these boys. He also organized excursions for them to the countryside and sometimes accompanied them on these expeditions — which was, no doubt, a considerable sacrifice of his time. He continued to give his services to Ponterotto until 1833, when the pressure of other engagements finally obliged him to resign.

On the Janiculum Hill which stands over St. Peter's Basilica there was a well-known retreat house, which was particularly favored by the Roman nobility and the upper classes as a place of preparation for their children before these made their First Communion. Enclosed retreats to selected groups were also conducted. At the beginning of the year 1823, Vincent was appointed director of retreats in this establishment, though he tried to avoid, not the task, but the designation.

Any sketch of Vincent Pallotti's work for youth would be incomplete without a reference to the part he played in the development of the first Roman night schools. Their originator was a woodcarver named Giacomo Casoglio, who from affection for his fellow artisans, conceived the design of collecting their children in the evenings in a large room located in the famous Via Giulia in the medieval quarter of Rome. This was in 1819. Nearby was a church dedicated to St. Nicholas and a Nocturnal Oratory was opened in the church in order to provide the religious part of the instructions of the pupils. Vincent Pallotti, from the beginning, shared in the work of this Oratory, as appears from his correspondence; in fact, the tenor of some of the letters shows that he was in charge of it, for we find him asking for help in fulfilling the schedules of the lectures and sermons. After the death of Casoglio, a Roman lawyer named Gigli took charge of the schools, and, always with the assistance of the Oratory, continued and extended the good work, for he erected two more schools. Gigli died heroically. During the cholera plague of 1837, he opened his house to the survivors of stricken homes and went from door to door, nursing and encouraging the frightened population, until he contracted the malady himself and died of it. The work was taken up where he left it by Vincent Pallotti, who not only reopened the existing schools when the cholera was over, but succeeded in creating a new one as well. He also managed to pay off all debts, and placed the institution on a sound financial basis by obtaining the support of benefactors who each paid a small monthly sum. He also obtained a fixed grant from the Treasury. When Vincent was obliged to leave Rome for a lengthy period after his breakdown in health in the year 1839, he resigned the direction of the schools into the hands of Msgr. (later Cardinal) Morichini, who retained it for some years till he was sent abroad as Nuncio. The Nocturnal Schools were again in need of a responsible leader; Vincent was appointed "Promoter"; this was in 1843. When Vincent Pallotti handed over the direction of the schools to Msgr. Morichini, there were one thousand pupils in eight establishments, the attendance being limited to boys who were precluded, by reason of their occupations, from attending the ordinary day schools. A contemporary writer thus described them:

"All school necessaries are supplied free by the Society. On Sundays and holidays the pupils meet principally for religious instruction and pious practices; and on the other days, the schools are open for an hour and a half, during which they are taught reading, writing, arithmetic, catechism, and sometimes the principles of design and geometry applied to the arts. At the close of the schools, the masters conduct the pupils in double file to their respective residences, chanting the Divine Praises...."

Vincent's participation in the Roman Night Schools leads us to reflect on an important characteristic of his apostolic work: his preoccupation with the revival of existing charitable works rather than the creation of new ones, unless these were absolutely necessary. He was always lending a hand to others,

buttressing their work, reorganizing and inspiring
new life into institutions which had fallen into decay.
An instance of this may be found in his work for the
Roman associations of artisans, known as the "Universities" of the tradesmen. These "Universities" were
the descendants of the medieval Guilds and right up
to the time of the first French occupation of Rome
had possessed much power in the regulation of
agriculture, trade and commerce; this power was at
length taken from them and vested in the state.
The "Universities" were religious as well as business
corporations; each one possessed its own church, had
its chaplain and its corporate religious exercises.
"Each art, or company of artists," writes Melia,
"had a church where only those of the same profession or business might assemble. These separate
congregations for artisans, having their own church
and their own statutes, were designated 'Universities,' and the young artisans were in a special
way watched over and instructed." The decay into
which the corporations fell, as a result of the state in-
terventions, extended also to the specifically religious
activities of these bodies. The religious authorities
sought to revive this aspect of the corporations and
Vincent Pallotti was called upon to reorganize them
from that point of view, a task which he proceeded
to perform with great enthusiasm. "He first," Melia
writes, "took in hand the 'university' of shoemakers.
For this purpose, he held the first meeting in the
Church of the Holy Ghost at the behest of the Vice-
Gerent of Rome. He had a spiritual retreat preached
to them and the reorganization of the university took
place at this small church by Ponterotto. To this,
succeeded that of the coachmen...then followed the
'university' of the bakers, and several other trades."

These manifold activities of Vincent Pallotti,
taken in conjunction with his position at the Roman
University and the spiritual direction of the Roman
Seminary, of which we will speak later, made his

daily life an extremely busy one. Simultaneously, he was much in demand as a confessor, so much so that he obtained leave from the ecclesiastical authorities to hear the confessions of men in the private chapel which he had been permitted to erect in his own home. He was also called frequently to assist people on their deathbeds, a spiritual service which at that time was much sought for by the people of Rome. Pallotti never failed to answer requests for this most charitable of all priestly tasks, even though, in some cases, it entailed not one, but several days' attendance on the departing soul.

Vincent did not, however, attempt to do everything himself. He had many friends among the secular and regular clergy and from his correspondence and the reminiscences of contemporaries, we learn that it was his practice to call upon them very freely for assistance, not only for the purpose of getting the work done, but also to make them sharers in the spiritual benefits of this active apostolate. Among the laity, too, he found willing assistance; people who provided him with religious objects for distribution, who gave him money for the relief of the needy, who on occasion, put their carriages at his disposal for journeys, especially at night. Here, too, he was moved to seek and accept collaboration, not precisely for its own sake, but because of the opportunity which it gave them of sharing in apostolic works of charity. In all this we may see foreshadowed the Society of the Catholic Apostolate which he was to found a few years later, whose purpose was to bring together like-minded persons of the secular and regular clergy, religious sisterhoods and the laity and coordinate their activities, spiritual and temporal, for apostolic purposes.

What of his own inner life, now that his external activity had become so absorbing? Without doubt, that most subtle of all temptations — activism — which has assailed so many pious men and women in their mature years, when success is attending their efforts and they realize that they can really get things done, must also have assailed Vincent. At this period there emerges in his Diary, with great force, the desire to identify himself and all his efforts with our Lord. This profound aspiration, which must be obtained first of all through God's grace humbly implored in prayer and freely imparted, and consolidated in the soul by the active imitation of the life of our Lord, was to stay with him till the end. He bequeathed it, as the most precious of legacies, to his spiritual followers. The rule of life he wrote for them is headed, chapter by chapter, with passages from the Gospels selected in such fashion as to relate their whole way of life to that of Christ on this earth and of His Mystical Body, the Church.

"So that Christ (he writes in his Diary) may be the true author of everything which proceeds from all my efforts, and particularly from the exercise of my sacred ministry, I will frequently say, especially when beginning any ministerial task: 'My Lord Jesus, expell me and put Yourself in my place; may my life be destroyed, and Your life be mine. I am unworthy of possessing the love of God. I am unworthy of the gift of exact compliance with my duties in my state of life and in fulfilling my obligations, but I ask most earnestly for this gift, through the mercy of God and the merits of Jesus. My God, I am not worthy of Your mercy and Your grace. My God, Your will be mine, Your life be mine. Mary Most Holy is the Teacher of the spiritual life; I am unworthy of her but I thank almighty God, who has given her to me for that end.'"

During his annual retreat for the year 1827, a hard year for him, because it was the year of his mother's death and his sensitive, affectionate spirit had suffered much during the long and painful process of her decline, he wrote the following in his Diary:

"May all my life be destroyed and may the life of Jesus alone be my life. May the life of Christ be my meditation and my study; may it be in me the ornament of the Church. May the prayer of Christ be my prayer, the word of Christ be my word, the love of Christ be my love, and the love of Christ for the Blessed Mother be my love for her."

The greatest of all religious works ever written by man, *The Imitation of Christ,* was always by his hand and he never failed to carry a copy on his person. When he waited on prelates and important personages and, as sometimes happened, had to spend much time in antechambers awaiting audience, the "Imitation" would be produced and he would become absorbed in it.

Vincent's manifold activities filled his contemporaries with admiration and his success in dealing with spiritual problems marked him in the minds of his ecclesiastical superiors as a man on whom they could rely, no matter how great the problem. In 1827 he was chosen by the Cardinal-Vicar of Rome for the post of spiritual director of the Roman Seminary. This appointment meant that on his shoulders fell a large share in the responsibility for the spiritual training of the future clergy of Rome, from whose ranks would emerge the future parish priests of the city, future bishops, papal diplomats, Cardinals, perhaps even future Sovereign Pontiffs. In the nature of things, the Roman Seminary had to be a model seminary, a headline for all such establishments in the rest of the world.

He undertook his duties there with great earnestness. Several times during the week he attended at the Seminary, where a room was placed at his disposal and he dealt with his charges unhurriedly, as though all the time in the world was at his command. With great sweetness he helped them to resolve not only their own personal problems, but taught them as well how to face up to the manifold difficulties which often confront clerics who from the nature of their sacred profession are destined to mingle with, though not to share in, the secular life of the world in which they must fulfill their vocation. For thirteen years Vincent was spiritual director of the Seminary until ill health in 1840 compelled him at last to withdraw. Many of his spiritual children, after they became priests, continued to avail themselves of his counsel and spiritual direction till his death.

Another famous institution for the training of priests in Rome is the great Propaganda College, where future missionaries for all parts of the world are prepared. In Pallotti's days the candidates were not drawn only from the Oriental peoples and the colored races of the earth. Among the inmates there was at this time a considerable contingent of Americans, Irishmen for dioceses in the British colonies and for the Irish mission itself, and other English-speaking aspirants. In the year 1833 the spiritual director of this establishment, who was in poor health, petitioned for an assistant and Vincent Pallotti was appointed. In practice, all the work fell upon his shoulders from the beginning; later, in 1835, he was formally appointed spiritual director of Propaganda and held the post till the college was handed over some years afterwards to the administration of the Jesuit Fathers. Here too he proceeded to attend the members of the college with the same care as in the Roman Seminary. His interest in foreign missions cannot be said, however, to date from this appointment, though no doubt it was stimulated by it; for Vincent Pallotti was mission-minded from the earliest days of his priesthood.

During this period of diversified spiritual works, strange things began to be whispered about this modest and unassertive young priest, who was always willing, and in fact always appeared pleased, to do the work and then stand aside and let others take the credit should they wish for it; who was not afraid of blame and reproach, indeed, in some mysterious fashion, had trained himself to welcome humiliations and contempt. People noticed that he slept very little and the report went around that he spent a good part of each night on his knees—which was quite correct —either praying or writing. The students of the Roman Seminary heard the report and now understood why he sometimes heard confessions on his knees and after each confession stood up or changed his posture. He was, in fact, overcoming sleep. There were other stories, too, of supernatural presciences: a youth whom he summoned from play to his room in the retreat-house in the Janiculum and induced to go to confession, in spite of the youth's good-humored protests that there was plenty of time the next day. But that night he died suddenly. Stories that one day in the confessional he seemed to fall into a trance and could not be awakened and later it became known that at the same time he was present at a deathbed in a distant part of the city; that, emerging from a trance during the Conclave in which Cardinal Capellari was elected Pope, he announced that this Cardinal had at that very moment been nominated, and the fact was confirmed an hour later by the public announcement; reports about counsels and advice which, he informed the interested parties, had been revealed to him through no human agency but by almighty God Himself; that, walking through storms of rain, his clothing remained completely dry; stories of unheralded appearances at deathbeds where his presence proved decisive in the conversion of some sinners. These things were whispered about him as he went his way through streets and alleyways: in later times witnesses were to come forward and give their evidence when the Cause of Beatification was opened.

Vincent knew that he was God's instrument for communication with certain people, for he states it quite clearly in letters which are still extant. He knew that certain extraordinary graces were offered him; he knew that God had more than once given him prescience; he must surely have known as well that prodigies were being performed by him as God's special agent. Knowledge of this kind must be a great and wonderful thing—and very terrible. An extract from his Diary tells us what he thought about himself even as he realized that he was a chosen instrument of the Divinity:

"My God, in all my works, how much evil have I done, how much good have I prevented, particularly in the exercise of my ministry and in public and private instructions! You alone know it! Against You alone have I sinned, and done evil before Your face. O my God, who knows how many souls have not advanced on the path of perfection or have been lost on my account! And yet my great, and indeed inconceivable vanity told me and led me to believe that I was doing good, and better than others! What an error, what madness, what a misconception! O my God, destroy all my past life, my present and my future, and give me Your life, the life of Your Incarnate only-begotten Son, and this life I offer You instead of my own. My God, I am an abyss of error, madness and misery. I must indeed confess that I do not know myself properly and thoroughly, and yet my self-esteem, which has always dominated me, has made me think that I knew myself. What a mistake! Help me, my God, help me! What I possess is not virtue but misery. I am the poorest being in the world in virtue; in misery I am indeed very rich, filled to overflowing. My God, my Mercy!"

It is a strange and wonderful passage and the reader is led on to reflect on that mysterious dispensation of God's Providence which lays down that the great graces granted to living mortals are always bound up with a great sense of humility and that the consciousness of sin is inescapable among Eve's fallen children, no matter how high the path they are treading through the sorrowful valley.

Two years previous to the foundation of the Society of the Catholic Apostolate, which must be regarded as Vincent's fundamental achievement, he printed and published his first work: a 154-page book dedicated to Our Lady Queen of Saints, and distributed in thirty daily readings, designed to be read by the religious leading a cloistered life. This leads us to refer to the sources and the nature of his devotion to our Blessed Lady, to defend whose Immaculate Conception he vowed himself in early life.

In the devotional context of Italian religious thought, the cultus of the Blessed Virgin has never appeared as a separate compartment of the spiritual life, as though the believer should have to pass from, say, the contemplation of God and Jesus Christ to something distinct and separate: our Lady, the angels, some favorite saint. The Blessed Virgin, as the Italians pray to her, is implicit in her Son, and the Son is implicit in our Lady. That is why Vincent Pallotti used to say that his favorite images of her were those in which she appeared with her Son in her arms, "because He is the reason of her."

Within this pattern of thought, we find in his spiritual writings, from the earliest to the last, that his references to our Lady are prefaced with a special formula, whose terminology may sound unusual to some of us: he writes of her as "my more than most beloved Mother." His words, wherever reference is made to our Lady, take on a certain vividness and a special color which show that we are in the presence of an unusual affection and tenderness of spirit. But these sentiments, far from terminating in themselves, are to be used in increasing the whole knowledge and the whole love of God.

"Devotion to our Lady" (he wrote in his retreat for the subdiaconate) "leads in reality to the imitation of her Son and to learning from her how to imitate Him. I will promote by all means in my power, the devotion of our Lady, my more than most beloved Mother."

The titles of our Lady fascinated him, and in his prayers he lingered lovingly over them. At one period, we find him invoking her as the Immaculate; at another period, she is entitled the Queen, at another, the Queen of Saints, at another, the Mother of Divine Love, at other times, the Powerful Virgin— *Virgo Potens;* and finally, the Queen of the Apostles, under which invocation, he dedicated the Society of the Catholic Apostolate.

"Writing or speaking of our Lady, particularly in preaching, I wish to give to the Blessed Virgin the most august titles. I am unworthy of loving our Lady, but by the mercy of God and the merits of Jesus Christ, I desire to obtain the grace of loving her, and it is my wish to love her with the very love which God has for her."

Perhaps the most important fact of all in the history of Vincent's devotion to the Blessed Virgin comes from an entry in his Diary, bearing the date of December 31, 1832. It is nothing less than Pallotti's account of his experience of that singular attachment which almighty God establishes through His grace between certain chosen souls and our Blessed Lady, which the spiritual writers designate with the title of espousals. The expression is founded on the doctrine, so firmly held and dearly loved by all Catholics, that no other human, or angelic being had ever attained, or can attain, so close and perfect a union with the Creator as the Blessed Virgin, even while she was still upon this earth. Her mind was rapt in the contemplation of the divinity, her will was wedded to the divine will in a type of union superior to, and stronger than even the union between body and soul in man and her whole being was flooded with an abundance of grace greater than that ever possessed by any other creature of God. The doctrine of the "espousals" lays down that in special instances almighty God permits other humans to be associated with Mary, and to share, through her, in that mystical union with the divinity.

Here are the words in Pallotti's Diary, in which he records this most wonderful of all experiences:

"On the last day of the year 1832, the great Mother of Mercy has by a miracle of mercy designed to triumph over the ingratitude and inconceivable unworthiness of this most wretched of all her existing or possible subjects in the kingdom of mercy. She has deigned to celebrate the spiritual espousals with him and has dowered him with all her possessions and has given him the knowledge of her divine Son; and she, being the spouse of the Holy Spirit, undertakes to transform him completely in the Holy Spirit. O, the mercy of Jesus, which is employed for the benefit of this ungrateful, wretched, unworthy, sacrilegious, sinful being, the most sinful who ever was or could possibly be, who nevertheless without delay heeds the request of the Mother! O, the mercy of Mary, the Immaculate Queen, who with such pity is moved to pray, intercede and obtain succor for this most wretched, ungrateful, sacrilegious sinner, the lowest of all in her kingdom of mercy! Paradise is filled with the mercies of Mary! I shall sing the mercies of the Lord forever. I shall sing the mercies of Mary forever. My God and my All."

Pallotti's devotion to our Lady is commemorated in a great many statues and pictures of him, in which he appears with an image of our Lady grasped in his extended palm. The attitude corresponds to historical reality. It was the common practice of the people at that time in Italy to kiss the hand of the priest when greeting him or bidding him farewell. Pallotti did not gladly fall in with this custom, but unable to avoid it completely, he had a special case made, enclosing an image of our Lady of Divine Love, which he always carried about with him, and when people attempted to kiss his hand, they found that this image was proffered instead.

He was indefatigable in distributing pictures and images of our Lady among the faithful. For years he was the chief client of an artisan who made his living by producing these objects; sometimes the entire production went into the hands of Vincent, later to be given out among the faithful. He felt that in thus propagating devotion to our Lady, he was fulfilling one of the great duties of the priesthood.

"Ecclesiastics must profess more than others, a special devotion to our Lady, for more than others they have learned the reasons for praising her, and also because their character and ministry is more similar to hers than that of others. More than other people, they stand in need of her intercession. My God, I am unworthy of perfect devotion to the Blessed Virgin, but You grant it to me through Your mercy and the merits of Jesus and Mary."

CHAPTER III

Foundation of the Society
of the Catholic Apostolate

The city of Rome has many claims for her pre-eminence among the great cities of the world; not least among them her position as the capital of the Catholic Church. Living at the center of this great hub of the universe, Vincent Pallotti was constantly meeting the missionaries who were traveling to and from the outposts of Catholicism; he thus became interested from early youth in the problems and the necessities of the far-away places where the banner of Christianity was being unfurled. He had a lofty conception of the duties incumbent on the clergy of Rome, who, as the immediate subjects of a universal Papacy, had therefore special obligations towards the support and encouragement of the missionaries throughout the world.

How to help the missionaries? He first began by supplying them, when they were setting out for the missions, with objects of piety: pictures, medals, scapulars and with furnishings for churches. In order to provide these objects he drew upon his friends and so a little association, quite unofficial, of helpers of the foreign missions came into being. Vincent was the life and soul of it. It was he who contacted the missionaries, found out what they needed and made the arrangements.

These benefactions embraced both the Eastern and the Western World. We find him arranging for sacred pictures for the diocese of New York, breviaries and oilstocks for the clergy of Philadelphia, plans for a church in Nova Scotia, help for the missionaries in Australia, financial assistance for the mission of New Zealand. He was equally interested in the work of the missionaries in the East, and when the graduates of the Propaganda were setting out for their posts he provided them with as much religious material for their work as he could collect. He also was concerned to send books and religious objects to the missionaries already in the field. With one such effort on his part, the origin of the Society of the Catholic Apostolate is indissolubly linked.

There was a missionary in the Middle East who needed ten thousand copies of "The Eternal Maxims" of St. Alphonsus in Arabic; he applied to Pallotti asking him to edit and pay for the edition. Four hundred Roman scudi, it was found on enquiry, would be needed; that is, about twelve hundred dollars in present-day currency. This request came in at the beginning of 1835.

In his own home Vincent Pallotti stored the pious objects and pictures which were later distributed, either personally or by the agency of friends. The house had become in time a sort of meeting-place for the little group of like-minded people who were seriously interested in advancing the cause of religion and piety. They were becoming concerned not only with the missionary field but with the needs of Catholicism everywhere, even in Rome itself. Some were priests, others laypeople. The priests were prepared to help Pallotti in all his undertakings, to teach catechism, to hear confessions when called upon, without prejudice to their other obligations; the laymen provided alms and personal services. These people were linked together by no other bond than their desire to do good in a practical way — and by their friendship and veneration for Vincent Pallotti. It was all completely voluntary; they were not a formal association; the group was nameless and as yet un-recognized by any authority.

At this stage in his interior life a supernatural interposition of Providence took place which St. Vincent Pallotti thus relates with great simplicity in his Diary:

"My God, my Mercy, in Your infinite mercy You grant me the task of promoting, establishing, propagating, perfecting and perpetuating (according to the most vivid desire of Your Sacred Heart) the following:

1. The creation of a universal apostolate among all Catholics for the propagation of the faith and the religion of Christ among infidels and non-Catholics;

2. Another apostolate for the revival, preservation and increase of faith among Catholics;

3. An institution of universal charity for the exercise of all the works of mercy, both spiritual and corporal, so that the knowledge of You, who are charity itself, may be spread as widely as possible. O my God, in Your presence, now and always, before the court of heaven, and before all beings, past, present and future, I confess that if until now such an institution has not been created, the fault lies with me, for You would not have denied me the graces had I made myself ready for them. In spite of my lack of the necessary dispositions, perhaps greater than ever now, I trust, in fact I know for certain, that the moment has arrived for a signal triumph of Your mercy over my lack of dispositions and unworthiness. My God, mercy and grace!"

The date was the 9th of January of the year 1835. The words in which Vincent states how he came to the knowledge of this new mission, this new orientation in his life, make it clear that he has been the recipient of a new and singular grace. "You grant me," he says; "I trust, in fact I know for certain."

It was at this very time the request for the Arabic edition of "The Eternal Maxims" came in. Under God's Providence, the two facts: the first, supernatural and in the inner order of grace; the other, an external fact in the ordinary established order of nature, are linked together.

A year before these events, Vincent Pallotti one day entered the home of a Roman shopkeeper named Giacomo Salvati, with whom he was not previously acquainted. The merchant was out, so Pallotti addressed Salvati's wife, who was in charge of the shop: "You sent for me?"

The lady answered in the negative, and then learned that the visitor's name was Pallotti; a name which she had heard mentioned with great respect, and she was much impressed by this unexpected call. As it happened, their eldest daughter was gravely ill in the house at that moment and the parents were much worried. She asked Vincent to pay a visit to the child, but Pallotti declined and left the house saying: "The girl will be all right." And so it was! In a few hours the disorder, whatever it was, disappeared completely to the puzzlement of the doctor in attendance, who was not afraid to use the word miracle to describe the happening.

From that moment the Salvati family could never do enough for Vincent and his charitable enterprises. When the request for the Arabic translation came in and Vincent ascertained the sum of money necessary to pay for it, he visited Salvati and asked him to collect it by visiting people here and there and asking for alms for the purpose. Salvati did not relish the task, but he took it on. At the last moment, just as he was due to set out on his distasteful errand he lost heart. He called on Pallotti instead and begged to be relieved of the task, alleging his incompetence and embarrassment, but Vincent declined to take these reasons into account. Finally Salvati agreed to set about it, but asked that Pallotti should give him a note saying that the collection was being made in the name of Vincent Pallotti, as a sort of guarantee of good faith, but again Vincent refused, saying "Ask in the name of Jesus Crucified."

Salvati complied, and to his great astonishment, people subscribed liberally; in a short time a considerable sum of money, larger than what was originally needed, was secured. It now became clear that a definite organization must be created to take charge and assume responsibility for the work and for the money, which was not subscribed at the request of any particular person. What followed can best be related in the words employed by Vincent himself, when he described the incident ten years later.

"In the year 1835 some people in Rome, moved by Christian charity, were anxious to print 'The Eternal Maxims' of St. Alphonsus in the Arabic tongue for the spiritual profit of the Catholics who use this language in the East. To this end a Roman priest encouraged a zealous layman to collect alms in order to pay for the printing and in a few hours, to his astonishment, he collected a considerable sum. In view of this, and in order to avoid exposing the good work to ill-natured criticism, it was thought convenient to create a Pious Society which, in the present state of necessity of the Church, would have for its purpose the multiplication of such spiritual and temporal aids, as are necessary and opportune for reviving faith and rekindling charity among Catholics and spreading these virtues throughout the world. It was not intended to create a new organization in the Church, but rather to revive the existing ones. In order to succeed, it was necessary to remove the barriers dividing the secular and the regular clergy and to inspire both of them with the spirit of charitable emulation and zeal, so that they might engage in the ministry ever more earnestly and according to modern methods, moved by an unselfish spirit and true humility, for the greater glory of God and the good of souls."

Vincent then goes on to state that it was also planned to encourage the laity of both sexes to share in the work, by prayers, by contributions of money and by personal service according to their trades or occupations. This union of the secular and regular clergy and laity of both sexes, all working together for the relief of spiritual and religious destitution, was to be organized and directed by a body of priests, living a community life and entrusted with the task of spreading the organization and the methods all over the world. This body of priests, or Congregation as he later called it, being placed half-way between the secular and regular clergy, was to serve as a bond of union between them. The Pious Union was to be designated "The Pious Society of the Catholic Apostolate, under the patronage of Our Lady Queen of Apostles." When, as time went by and their specific functions became more clearly defined, the directing priests of the organization became known as "The Congregation of Priests of the Catholic Apostolate."

In order to evaluate Vincent's plan and his achievement it is first of all necessary to bear in mind that there was a great number of apostolic institutions already existing in Rome; he himself belonged to many of them—as we have seen: schools, hospitals, organizations for youths, for seminarians, for clergy, and so on. Many of them were "Pious Unions," that is, organizations dedicated to some religious purpose to which ecclesiastical recognition had been extended and the rules of association approved, in which the members did not by the fact of association change their status; the secular or regular clergyman who joined did not change his state; nor did the layman who gave in his name.

The population of Rome, taken at modern standards, was not great. At the beginning of the nineteenth century its population was 153,000 and at the height of the Napoleonic occupation in 1813, it had fallen to 117,000. After that date it began to rise again; by 1857 it had climbed to 178,000. Rome today has a population of two million. During the lifetime of Vincent Pallotti, the percentage of ecclesiastical persons, including priests, seminarians and religious of both sexes was about three per cent of the population; fifty years earlier it had been as high as five per cent. These are considerable percentages by any standard, and may be explained by the fact that Rome, being the seat of the central administration of the

Catholic Church and of the headquarters of the religious Orders and congregations, possessing too an exceptional number of great churches and basilicas with extensive staffs, numerous seminaries and clerical institutions of learning, has special requirements for religious personnel.

We must therefore take into account, in assessment of Pallotti's apostolic plan, the presence of a large clerical and religious element in the city who were for the most part occupied, each in his own place, in various institutionalized activities which were regulated by dispositions and customs coming down from early times. They were little affected by the ferment of change which had seized on the civilian population in whose midst they lived—a ferment which was compounded of many elements, including the anti-clericalism, irreligion and blind hatred of the Church and of all religious values which characterized the secret societies of the era.

There is a further element in this ferment, also worthy of note: the lingering Jansenistic taint which had filtered down into Italy and was not yet dead, even in Rome itself. For most people who have just skimmed the subject, the word Jansenism signifies a certain rigorist attitude in morals, a certain exaggerated theory of general ascetics, involving the repudiation of frequent Communion and a low opinion of the average person's chances of eternal salvation. But Jansenism was much more than this. It had its own theory of church government and particularly of the function of the religious orders. These, they said, should be limited in numbers and excluded from pastoral ministry, which ought to be the exclusive prerogative of the secular clergy.

These theories seeped into Italy during the eighteenth century. Groups of Jansenistically-minded clergy and laity appeared in Liguria, in Brescia and notably in Tuscany, where, at the end of that century, a famous Synod was held at Pistoia, whose tenets were later solemnly condemned by the Holy See. But a long period was to elapse before the spirit behind this movement finally died out. Pallotti's principle that the Society of the Catholic Apostolate must form a link between both branches of the clergy and excite each of them towards greater apostolic activity among the people must therefore be regarded as a contribution to the liquidation of practical Jansenism, which had raised its head even in Rome. His insistence too that the Society should be placed under the absolute and immediate dependence of the Holy See must also be regarded as contrasting with the Jansenistic theory of the Church: a theory which attempted to over-emphasize the position of the individual bishops—and of the rulers of the states where they were located—at the expense of the Holy See. And finally Pallotti's life-long advocacy of the devotion to the Sacred Heart of our Lord can, apart from its warm ascetical and devotional content, be regarded as yet another repudiation of the theory of Jansenist spirituality.

Vincent's first step, after his spiritual experience of January 9, 1835, was to call his occasional collaborators and determine how many of them were prepared to follow him in the constitution of the new Society. A list was drawn up, in which as was stated earlier, the first name was that of Fazzini, Vincent's spiritual director, and the second, Vincent's own. There follow thirteen more names, among them several laymen. Two of the priests were members of an Eastern Rite.

The next step was to obtain ecclesiastical approval for the Society, without which it could not exist. A document setting forth the purposes of the new organization was submitted to the Cardinal-Vicar of Rome, Cardinal Odescalchi (the saintly prelate who a few years later was to resign all his titles and enter the Society of Jesus, where he died with the reputation of sanctity) on April 4, 1835. The

statement, which is brief, lays down that several
Roman priests and lay people propose to unite in
order to gather spiritual and material resources for
the propagation of the faith and for charitable purposes. They wish, the document goes on to say,
to dedicate their society to Our Lady Queen of
Apostles and suggest that its title should be "The
Catholic Apostolate." The good Cardinal immediately
granted his blessing to the undertaking. This date
has always been kept as the birthday of the Society.
The next step was to publish a statement, addressed
to the Catholics of Rome, explaining the aims and
ideals of the new organization. This document contains the following statement:

> "This Association, by means of the evangelical action,
> part of it, but also of all those who assist it if only on a single
> occasion, will endeavor to awaken the faith and piety of
> Christians and to multiply the means of preserving and
> propagating the Catholic religion."

Observe the phrase "evangelical action"; there
is a contemporary ring about it. In our time we have
become familiar with the word "action" as applied
to organized movements towards an ideal type of
society; in the term "Catholic Action" it has been
spread over the whole world. We have grown accustomed as well to speaking and hearing of "activ-
ists," whether in the Catholic field, or far outside it.

Vincent's next step was an application to the Vice-
Gerent of Rome, that is, the next ecclesiastical superior ranking after the Cardinal-Vicar. This was
Archbishop Piatti, an old friend with whom Vincent
had collaborated for years in the retreat-house on the
Janiculum Hill. His blessing too was obtained. And
finally, most important step of all, Vincent approached
the Holy Father in person. The petition, which was
presented to the Sovereign Pontiff by the Cardinal-
Vicar, states categorically (the petition to the Cardinal-
Vicar merely carried a tentative suggestion to this

effect) that the title of the Society is "the Pious Union of the Catholic Apostolate, erected in Rome under the patronage of the Queen of the Apostles." The Holy Father's rescript, written at the foot of the petition, states that "His Holiness concedes a thousand blessings to the Society of the Catholic Apostolate, and also to all the works of piety and zeal which the Society is to undertake." This document bears the date July 11, 1835.

Now that we are in possession of the details and circumstances surrounding the foundation of the Society of the Catholic Apostolate, we will retreat a little in the order of time and deal with another event in the life of Vincent Pallotti which had a considerable bearing on the early history of the Society. This was his appointment as Rector of the Church of the Holy Ghost, situated on the Via Giulia, in the heart of Old Rome.

About three years after his ordination to the priesthood Vincent Pallotti in his Spiritual Diary registers the following vow:

"Not to accept dignities, but to leave such matters in the hands of my spiritual director; and hence, never to accept any without his permission and absolute consent."

It is on record that on two occasions his ecclesiastical superiors made offers of this kind to Vincent. The first time was in 1829, when he was offered a canonry in the collegiate Chapter of the Church of Our Lady *Ad Martyres* better known to all tourists and visitors to Rome under the name of the Pantheon. Vincent declined. The second time was in 1833, when the Cardinal-Vicar offered him the post of parish priest of St. Mark's, the beautiful church which forms part of the structure of the famous Palazzo Venezia. This, too, he declined and we may be certain that in both cases he was acting on the counsel of his spiritual director.

Another offer was made to him in the course of the year 1834. The church of the Holy Spirit was erected in the sixteenth century for the use of the Neapolitan residents in Rome and belonged to the category of "national" churches, of which there were a large number in the Eternal City. The Florentines, the Venetians, the natives of Lucca and other communities originating from the independent states into which Italy was then divided, all possessed "national" churches in Rome. In many cases the appointments for these churches were in the gift of the ruler of the state concerned; this was the case with the church of the Holy Spirit of the Neapolitans, to which the King of Naples, still on his throne, had the right of making nominations on the clerical and lay staff. It had, however, become the practice for the temporal ruler to make these appointments, in the case of clerics, in concert with the Roman ecclesiastical authorities.

The church of the Holy Spirit was situated in a very populous area and it offered plenty of scope for apostolic activities. There were several clergymen occupying minor posts in the service of the church, and drawing their emoluments accordingly, and there were servants to look after the upkeep and maintenance of the building. It appears that the general atmosphere of the place was not what it should be: the clergy did not welcome the attendance of people in church, lest demands be made on their time; the servants did not want people coming around the place, for it meant having to keep the church neat and clean, and this made inroads on leisure which could be more pleasantly spent otherwise. Decidedly the church of the Holy Spirit was run down, and the Roman Vicariate decided to put new life into it. Vincent Pallotti was asked to become the Rector, and he accepted. Once more we can be certain that he did so only after consultation and on the advice of his spiritual director.

The Church of the Holy Spirit provided him with a field of apostolic activity similar to that in which he had been working for fifteen years, in a number of churches and institutions. The church now placed in his charge was just another place which needed to be "revived." But in the background of his mind, the idea of a society "for the revival of faith and charity" was already taking shape. Further, the Rector of the church was entitled to a set of rooms in the rectory next to the church. The establishment of a community dedicated to the service of his ideal had not hitherto been concretely possible. At this point he is offered this church and the facilities of its rectory. It was another pointer from divine Providence showing him the road he was to follow.

His spiritual Diary for this period of his life (1832-1836) informs us not only of these extraordinary graces and communications from God to which we have already referred—the spiritual espousals with our Lady, the certitude of God's call on him to found the Society of the Catholic Apostolate. The Diary speaks of other communications too. For instance, after the celebration of Mass on January 9, 1835, he writes of "the innumerable and inconceivable mercies which you bestowed on me."

Extraordinary graces granted to human beings may entail extraordinary demands on the recipients. On the date given above, Vincent Pallotti asks God for a special favor which will enable him to face up to any such demands:

"My God, I believe indeed that your mercies have not been abbreviated; I believe with all certitude that they are now commencing for me. The first example of your mercy which I ask for is that among your creatures there may be found one, which possessed of your spirit will despise me, chastise me, strike me, humiliate me so as to bridle my evil passions, particularly my pride .... The other mercy which I ask is that, through sufferings, torments, and martyrdoms without end and without measure and without number, you may bestow on me whatever is necessary to destroy every sin and every evil in the world which has ever existed or could exist, and that I may be able to promote every good in all the world, now and forever."

Self-inflicted mortifications and penances there are many in Vincent's life, and we have seen that he had been practicing them from early youth. But he now feels the necessity, in view of the marvelous graces he had received, of securing some addition to them from external sources, and God is asked to provide these sources.

The subsequent history of his tenure of the rectorship of the church of the Holy Spirit and the troubles experienced during the early days of the Society of the Catholic Apostolate, go to show that the special favor of external humiliation which he asked of God in the passage just cited, was indeed granted!

Vincent's tenure of the rectorship of the church of the Holy Spirit meant that, quite suddenly, large numbers of people began frequenting a building which almost nobody entered before. People came for confessions and spiritual direction, for the novenas and pious exercises which he instituted, for the Masses in the mornings. People came to receive alms and to bestow them, to seek recommendation in order to obtain work, to find places for orphans in some home, or just to see him and pray in the same church in which he was praying. The place became a hive of movement. This did not please the clergy and the servants, whose comfort was disturbed by these crowds of people, and they bore it ill. Their lamentations, their protests and their counter-measures did not however become unusually outrageous till Vincent himself went to live in the Rector's rooms after the death of his father in 1837.

Vincent's earliest biographer, Father Raphael Melia, was an eyewitness of the treatment which was meted out to him during these years at the church of the Holy Spirit:

"He was forbidden to hear confessions, and to allow people to go to confession, in the evenings; no functions were permitted in the church; then it was kept open only a few hours in the morning; finally all the confessionals were removed from it. At times, Vincent was obliged to take off his vestments just when he was about to celebrate Mass; there was sometimes no water, sometimes no wine; sometimes the candles were so fixed that they went out during Mass. The keys of the church and sacristy were taken from him; he was forced to give up the keys of some of the rooms inhabited by the priests (of the Society) — rooms to which he was entitled as rector — and forced to pay a rent for them."

There came a time when the exasperation of his petty persecutors reached the extremity that one of them struck him in the presence of several witnesses. And finally an attempt was made to drive him out altogether. But one of Vincent's collaborators, without his knowledge, appealed to a Cardinal who immediately went to see the Holy Father and acquaint him with this sorry state of affairs. The result was an intervention by the Secretary of State who ordered that Vincent was not to be molested any more in this fashion and that he must have entire liberty to carry out his work. His companions noticed that all through this petty persecution, which lasted for several years, he never complained, never took counter-measures, and uniformly showed himself cheerful and unaffected by the constant pin-pricks and small insults, which can be all the more aggravating when they are long-repeated and purposeful.

The group opposed to him and to his fellow-priests of the Society was made up by some of the Neapolitan priests attached to the church and the servants who possessed certain vested rights in virtue of their nominations by the King of Naples. These rights were of course religiously respected by Vincent, but the new situation of the church as a center of popular worship and devotion became more and more irksome to them. They appealed to the Patron, the King of Naples, who ordered an investigation into the charges and found that they were completely unfounded, but as Vincent himself refused to complain about his persecutors, nothing was done to remove them from their places or to prevent them effectively from continuing to act as they had been doing.

There was a sequel. Years after Vincent's death, one of the ring-leaders in this ugly little cabal was still alive and was called as a witness in the Process of Vincent's Beatification. In his deposition he stated:

"I feel within myself devotion and veneration for the Servant of God, for I have been a witness of his virtue, particularly his charity and meekness.... I can state that during the period when he was Rector everything was in perfect order.... I also observed in him humility and suffering.... The priests of his community not only did not inconvenience me and the other priests of the kingdom of Naples, but in the cause of truth I must even say that the Neapolitan priests made trouble for the Servant of God.... I have seen him, even in the midst of tribulations, preserving peace of mind and subjecting himself to God's dispositions. He was cautious, exact, diligent and circumspect in his mode of acting. I also state that he gave no cause or motive to be insulted.... In speaking with me I have remarked the great respect with which he treated me...."

The facts about Vincent's persecution became known in ecclesiastical circles, though not because he divulged the matter, and his contemporaries bore it in mind. Years afterwards, when Fr. St. John of the Birmingham Oratory interviewed the Prefect of Propaganda, regarding the treatment which was being meted out to Cardinal Newman, the Prefect made this observation: "Saints are always persecuted; *like Pallotti.*"

The investigation made at the request of the King of Naples was not sufficiently thorough, but some years after Vincent's death another inquiry was made and the truth came out. The church was well-endowed but the revenues had been carelessly administered for many years. Vincent, under the terms of his appointment as Rector, was excluded from all responsibility for the financial administration, but his presence, and that of his community, in the clergy-house was no doubt a considerable embarrassment to the careless administrators. When the second inquiry was completed, the unjust stewards were all compelled to resign.

The Church of the Holy Spirit was the first headquarters of the Society of the Catholic Apostolate. The year after the foundation, Vincent decided that the progress of the Society could be better insured if independent premises were found where the headquarters might be established, and he did in fact take steps towards acquiring a house for this purpose, but the necessary funds were not forthcoming. Meanwhile, the rooms at the church of the Holy Spirit were at his disposal (for the persecution outlined above had not yet taken the form of trying to deprive him of them) and in 1837 Fr. Melia and other priests took up residence there, the means of their maintenance being supplied by Vincent, who joined them as soon as the death of his father left him free to withdraw from the family home. In the rector's rooms the little group lived a community style of life. Some of those who came to live in the rectorate did so with a view of joining the Catholic Apostolate; others were preparing themselves for missionary work abroad.

As was remarked earlier in our story, Vincent Pallotti was always missionary-minded. He was deeply interested in recruiting priests and ecclesiastical students for this great ideal and his duties in the Propaganda College served to increase his enthusiasm. The Propaganda College was by its statutes closed to Italian secular students aspiring to serve on the foreign missions and there was not in Rome any establishment at that time where such aspirants could be accommodated. If a foreign missionary college, open to Italians, could be created, how much good could be done! Vincent considered that such a college should be situated in Rome, for he had much esteem for the training provided there and he felt that "the Roman spirit," rich in liturgical expression and in popular devotion, would be a great advantage to any missionary. He decided that the Society of the Catholic Apostolate should take the initiative in founding a College of this sort. In the year 1838 he drew up a plan, conceived in very general terms, for this purpose. The entire project was to be placed under the direct dependence of the Holy See.

"The supreme Catholic Apostolate (he writes) has been communicated by our Lord to the Sovereign Pontiff.... In order that any mission may be successful, it is necessary that the Pope, as the supreme apostle, must grant a legitimate mission, that is, the true, Catholic Apostolate to men of proved vocation, who in order to correspond to so high a vocation, should attend some well-ordered College where they can acquire the spirit and the doctrine necessary to carry out their sublime vocation; so that, imbued with the doctrines of St. Peter and of the Roman See, they may spread abroad the treasures of the Catholic, Apostolic and Roman Church."

The congregation of Propaganda Fide, under whose jurisdiction the missionaries would be eventually placed, was not unwilling to entertain the proposal, but it made clear its wish that the new college should be endowed before commencing operations. Vincent Pallotti was at this same time engaged in collecting funds for the two charitable institutions which he had just erected in the city of Rome and was not, personally, in a position to secure much financial aid towards the endowment of a college, which would require a very large sum. His apartments in the church of the Holy Spirit of the Neapolitans continued to keep its doors open to intending missionaries, but the project did not develop along the lines he had envisaged. Hope revived in his breast when, in 1841, the Superior of the Greek College in Rome, who was an old friend of Vincent's, proposed that this college, which was undergoing a severe financial crisis and had plenty of room for students, could be made available for missionary students of the Latin rite, so long as a certain number of Greeks, with a chaplain of their own, would be maintained on the foundation. For a while it seemed as if the missionary plan would now be brought to a successful conclusion, but in the end financial and other considerations—including the efforts of what Vincent characterized as "God's enemy"—prevailed, and so this plan fell through. But the idea that his Society should play a part in training missionaries remained fixed in his mind. Two years before his death, having learned that a fairly large income was about to pass, under the terms of a will, to the Holy See for charitable purposes, he drew up an application to the Holy Father, praying that this income should be applied to the support of a missionary college, because the creation of such an institution was one of the reasons why the Society had been founded. Though Providence had disposed that Vincent himself was not to succeed in establishing a college of missionaries within the Society during his lifetime, he had some share in the foundation of four great enterprises, which to this day continue to enlarge the frontiers of the Catholic religion in the missionary regions.

The first of these is the Subiaco Congregation of the Benedictine Order, which was organized by Dom Peter Casaretto OSB. He was in Rome in the year 1845, taken up with his plan of forming a branch of the Benedictine Order where the Rule of St. Benedict would be taken in its original sense, that is, without reference to the mass of later legislation which, in the course of the centuries, had grown up around the primitive code. For this reason, the congregation which Abbott Casaretto eventually created, first became known as "The Primitive Observance." During his stay in Rome, Abbott Casaretto selected Vincent Pallotti for his spiritual director and one important result of the association was that Casaretto decided to enlarge his ideal of a "primitive observance" of the Rule of St. Benedict, by adding a special concern for the Foreign Missions. The evidence for this is provided by Casaretto himself, who, writing to the Rector-General of the Society after Vincent's death, stated the following:

"In the month of July of the year 1846 I obtained from the Congregation of Propaganda Fide leave to found a monastic seminary for the Foreign Missions in the Monastery of St. Julian, obliging ourselves to train the young monks in the primitive observance of St. Benedict and at the same time in the ministry of the apostolic missions. I was encouraged to undertake this holy task by my good director, Vincent Pallotti, whom I had the misfortune to lose by his recent death in Rome."

The Monastery of St. Julian near Genoa soon filled up with young monks; among them four Englishmen sent by Archbishop Polding from Great Britain. In 1850, on the advice of Pius IX, the monastery was removed from Genoa to Subiaco. When Abbott Casaretto decided to establish a branch of his Observance in England, Vincent heard about his intention, and wrote to Melia in London to do everything in his power to assist him. Eventually the Subiaco Congregation established the great Abbey of Ramsgate in England. The Benedictine missionaries founded by Abbott Casaretto are working now in many of the mission-fields of the Catholic Church: in India and the Far East, in the Americas, in Australia and other places.

The second missionary enterprise which shared in Vincent's inspiration is the Foreign Missionary Society in Milan. Among the earliest recruits for his proposed missionary college whom Pallotti received in his apartments at the church of the Holy Spirit was a certain Giuseppe Marinoni, a young secular priest who wished to train as a missionary. He spent several years in Vincent's company, sharing in all the activities of the Society of the Catholic Apostolate. A diffident man, he was advised by Vincent to dedicate himself for a while to pastoral work in a parish in Rome and a place was found for him as a curate. Eventually he returned to Milan where he helped to organize the great Milanese missionary society. It is not quite clear if he was the actual founder; he was, in any case, the first Rector of the missionary college, a post which he held for a great many years. It is pleasant to recall that having learned in his old age that the Society of the Catholic Apostolate had founded in Piedmont a missionary college for members of the community, he paid a visit to the establishment and recalled with affection and veneration his first spiritual leader. He was also able to provide important evidence, arising from his long association with Vincent, for the Process of Beatification.

In the early months of 1842 an Irish priest, destined to be long-remembered, came to Rome seeking approval for a missionary college which he had established in Dublin. This was Fr. John Hand, alumnus of Maynooth College who was ordained in Dublin at the end of 1835, worked for some years in conjunction with the Irish Vincentian Fathers and then developed a deep interest in the Society for the Propagation of the Faith. He was concerned in particular with the spiritual perils to which so many Irish emigrants were exposed in those days, and in order to meet an evident and pressing need he decided to found a College in Ireland where young men could be trained for the secular missionary priesthood, for service in the dioceses which were being organized in the missionary countries. His project was approved by the Irish Bishops, but since the countries where the alumni would go to work lay within the juris- diction of Propaganda, he came to Rome to secure the approval of that organization. On the 3rd of February he presented his petition to Cardinal Fransoni, Prefect of the Propaganda; approval was granted on the 28th of the same month. Fr. Hand spent the interval "calling on everyone (writes his biographer) he knew or heard of as having influence." He certainly got in touch with Pallotti, for a couple of weeks afterwards an Appeal, drawn up in the French language and calling for donations for the Missionary College of All Hallows, Dublin, was published in Rome. It bears Vincent Pallotti's signa- ture.

And finally there is Vincent's posthumous share in the foundation of St. Joseph's Missionary Society at Mill Hill. In the life of Cardinal Vaughan, we read that this prelate, before he became a bishop, spent a holiday with Cardinal Wiseman in the Isle of Wight in the year 1860. One day they went driving together, and Vaughan addressed the Cardinal on a subject which was very near his heart:

"I asked him whether he had any interest in foreign missions. 'Yes, why do you ask?' he said. 'Because I have something on my mind and I fear to tell you...I believe England ought to do something for the foreign missions,' said I... 'Then I will tell you...' he replied. 'I have never yet told this to any one; but the time, I believe, has come. When I was in Rome before my consecration I had great mental troubles, and I went to a holy man, since dead and declared Venerable (Vincent Pallotti). He made me sit at one side of a little table; he sat on the other. A crucifix was on the table between us. After I had opened my mind to him and laid bare all its trials, he slipped down from his chair to his knees, and after a moment's prayer said: "Monsignor, you will never know the perfect peace you seek until you establish a College in England for the Foreign Missions." These words fell on me like a thunderbolt; I was in no way prepared for them. I had no interest at the time in foreign missions, nor had the Abbate Pallotti. He gave no other answer to my difficulties.... I then made a resolution to try to form a society of priests who should establish a College for foreign missions. On reaching England I at once explained my plans to Dr. Walsh. He opposed them definitively and said that Oscott was to be my foreign missionary college.... I had no choice but to obey.... I determined to wait till the person who should undertake it should be presented to me and never to let a day pass without praying to know God's will and His time for its execution. You are the first person who has offered himself for the purpose. I am now old and cannot hope to do much myself, but I see that God has answered my prayers and that the work is from Him.'"

Cardinal Wiseman's episcopal consecration took place in 1840; his recollection is therefore at fault when he stated that Pallotti did not have at that time any interest in foreign missions. He also appears to have forgotten that in 1849 he was endeavoring to establish a foreign missionary college in England, and that he was anxious to have Pallotti come to England to help him in the enterprise. This fact emerges from a letter written by Vincent to Melia in May 1849, which contains the following paragraph:

"I rejoice greatly in God that Mgr. Wiseman wishes to establish the missionary college; an enterprise which requires us to aim our souls against the Enemy. Therefore, let us submerge ourselves in the abyss of our nothingness and indignity, and God will do everything; I admire the virtuous trust of the good prelate, who desires that I should go there and I admire the works of God. Should God desire it, He will arrange everything so that I can go, but at present I cannot go, and in any case if God does not will it, I can at least be sure that God does not desire to use me as an impediment to the good work. The house which the Bishop possesses four miles from London, should be secured...."

This effort came to nothing. Cardinal Wiseman was destined to wait till Herbert Vaughan sought his support ten years later and Pallotti's original recommendation was finally fulfilled through the patience, the sacrifices and the great organizing ability of Vaughan and his helpers.

Let us return now to the vicissitudes of the Society of the Catholic Apostolate in the days just after its foundation. People soon appeared who objected to the title which Vincent had bestowed on the Society: a title which had already been accepted by the ecclesiastical authorities of Rome, and above all, by the Sovereign Pontiff, in the terms of the Rescript which we quoted earlier. The objection was based on the consideration that no one society in the Catholic Church was entitled to call itself "The *Catholic* Apostolate," for only the Church is Catholic, and only her apostolate as a whole can be described as "Catholic." Pallotti and his friends, it was urged, had no right to appear as if claiming for themselves the entire apostolate of Christ's Church. Now, had it been Vincent's intention to found a society for the purpose of taking over the supreme apostolate of the Catholic Church, or even the total apostolate in any particular diocese or parish, the objectors would have been quite right. But he had no such intention, any more than St. Ignatius when founding the Society of Jesus, meant to set up an exclusive claim to the person of our Lord. This is what was pointed out to Melchior Cano, whose great theological learning did not save him from confusing the issue in that very fashion.

Vincent hastened to explain his selection of the title in the following clear terms:

"The Society is called 'The Catholic Apostolate,' not because it presumes to possess for itself the Catholic

Apostolate, that is, the Catholic Mission of the true Church of Christ, but because it venerates this Apostolate, respects and loves it, and desires that it should be helped by everybody; in the same sense that other pious institutions are said to belong to some Saint, or to Jesus, or the Redeemer, not because it is intended to convey that the institution has an exclusive title to the Saint to whom it is dedicated, or to the person of our Lord or the Redeemer, but rather that they have been founded in honor of our Lord or the Redeemer.

"The Society of the Catholic Apostolate has been founded to stimulate all classes of persons, everywhere, to contribute in all possible ways to the revival of faith and charity among Catholics and to propagate these values among unbelievers."

When a misunderstanding has once arisen and has led responsible people astray, it is not easy to track it down and clear it up, particularly when the error has not acquired public status and is being carried merely from mouth to mouth. This was the predicament of Vincent and his associates, who were placed on the defensive and were forced to seek out opportunities to explain the truth of the situation. Error is hard to track to its lair. It appeared at one moment that the title "Catholic Apostolate" might have to be abandoned because the opposition to it was too powerful. Prudence suggested, while the question was still open, that the secondary title of the Society, based on the invocation of "Our Lady Queen of the Apostles" had better be employed. For a considerable time Vincent abstained from using the title "Society of the Catholic Apostolate" whenever the circumstances might revive or exasperate the zeal of his adversaries.

The point at issue has been clarified by the march of time. For decades now the Church has been served by an organization whose official title is "Catholic Action," which has been blessed, approved and enforced by several Popes and by the bishops of the Catholic world, and no one would now dream of asserting that the organization known as Catholic Action has superseded, or even attempted to take over the efforts (that is, the "action") of the other Catholic organizations which preceded it or have come into existence since then.

The secondary title of Vincent Pallotti's foundation: the Society under the patronage of "Our Lady Queen of the Apostles" must be examined with much interest by anyone who wishes to know the true spirit of the organization created by Vincent Pallotti. It is a fact that the founder himself used it as an alternative. It would be a mistake to think that it was chosen much as proper names are selected, by reason of some antecedent attachment to that particular invocation; or because of some extrinsic connection between the name and the object. Shakespeare's famous observation about the rose and its name can be verified whenever there is a question of names which are no more than sounds, but when there is a question of names which in themselves have a significance of their own, and these names are then employed to designate specific objects, the matter must further be inquired into. We have remarked above that Vincent Pallotti used many titles in his form of addressing our Lady, and over some of them he lingered with loving insistence, but it is noteworthy that "Queen of Apostles" does not occur among them till the foundation of the Society had taken place. It is also to be borne in mind that the mystical experience known as the spiritual espousals, on which we have also commented earlier, immediately preceded, according to the order established in his Diary, the divine communication regarding the founding of the Society. Is there not reason to conclude that his use of the new invocation, which became ever more and more frequent, is related to both these experiences — is in fact the connecting link between them?

The invocation of our Lady as Queen of Apostles, containing as it does in one formula Vincent's often-expressed conception of our Lady as Queen and the nature of the apostolic ideal which he wished all his followers to possess — has a deeper significance for his disciples. In the great prayer which he drew up for recitation, not only by the members of his community, but by all the associates of his work, he confirms the same idea and stresses this significance. This prayer, which is addressed to the Queen of the Apostles, contains a petition that our Lady shall obtain the graces of the Apostolate for all the members and associates of the Society and the merits of the works performed are offered to God through the medium of our Lady. The Society of the Catholic Apostolate is to operate through Mary and it is therefore, in the mind of its founder, a *Marian* Society, and the secondary title is designed as well as the primary one, to express the nature of that Society.

We will refer now to a second complication which cropped up in the path of the Catholic Apostolate. Vincent wished that the members of the Society should display activity not only in the local problems which surrounded them, but should be zealous for the foreign missions. This zeal was to be expressed not only by cooperating in the erection of a college for foreign missionaries, as we have seen earlier, but also in the periodical collection of small sums of money, which were to be handed in to Propaganda for the purposes of that institution.

There was a pre-existing example of the success of efforts of this kind. In the year 1819 a young Frenchwoman named Pauline Jaricot living in Lyons persuaded her companions to give her a penny a week for the support of missionaries and then organized a system for collecting the money and sending it on to its destination. The plan took hold with surprising rapidity and in a short time the Lyons Society for the Propagation of the Faith had spread all over the world.

In the year 1835 Pauline Jaricot stayed in Rome and met Pallotti, with whom she talked about her system. Next year Vincent utilized the services of his Associates of the Catholic Apostolate along those lines too; money for the missions began to flow in. Somebody however was not pleased to see the Society of the Catholic Apostolate performing this good work, which though it was being done by others elsewhere, was not being done by anyone in Rome till Vincent set about it. This displeasure was soon to lead to unpleasant consequences for him and his companions.

CHAPTER IV

Vincent's Society Under Trial

The opportunity for an all-out onslaught against
the Society of the Catholic Apostolate was provided
when the Sovereign Pontiff decreed in 1837 that a
branch of the work of the Propagation of the Faith
after the Lyons model should be set up in Rome. A
meeting was held in the presence of the Cardinal-
Prefect of Propaganda and it was decided to use the
machinery of the organization which Vincent had
created for the purpose of taking up the collections
of the new Roman branch of the Propagation of the
Faith. Vincent was asked to suggest the names for
the membership of the new Council. Cardinal Brignoli, a warm supporter of the Catholic Apostolate,
became the President and four members of the
Society, including Vincent himself, were nominated
on the Council.

The arrangement did not work, chiefly because
the "opposition" wanted the Society thrust out of
the work altogether, even though, in the short period
that it performed its task under the auspices of the
Lyons organization, it was quite successful in gathering funds and securing popular support. One of the
ways in which the Society could be removed from its
position in the missionary effort of the Propagation
of the Faith in Rome would be to destroy it altogether!
Influences were mobilized, pressures were exerted,
the aid of those who did not approve of the title of
the Society was sought, and finally on July 30, 1837,
the Secretary of Propaganda, who was an old friend
of Vincent, sought him out to show him privately a

copy of the Decree which had been prepared, suppressing the Society of the Catholic Apostolate completely. He found Vincent in the sacristy of a Roman church, where he was assisting at a meeting of people called for the purpose of selecting a President and Secretary for a new branch of the Propagation of the Faith which had just been set up in that parish. In the presence of them all, the Secretary handed Vincent the letter, and withdrew.

It was a dramatic moment. Not only were years of work and sacrifices on the point of being nullified, but the very validity of his execution of the interior command received that morning of January, 1835, seemed to be placed in doubt.

"An event so sudden (writes Melia, his earliest biographer), never to be expected by Vincent, nay, not even imagined, could not but produce the most profound impression upon his sensitive heart, for he loved the Pious Society. And yet in reading this document Vincent was not disturbed or discomposed; he gave not so much as a sigh, made no complaint; he only raised his eyes to heaven to thank the Lord, and he cast them down upon the ground, reverencing His most adorable will. Without interrupting the business which was being treated, he pursued with the same firmness of will and placidity of action, the promotion of that same work which demanded the destruction of the Society."

Present on this occasion was a Father Togni, Superior General of the Order of St. Camillus, famous in his day and remembered in our own time because he is the author of a manual which students in Rome preparing for the Minor Orders are still expected to study. Father Togni made this comment: "I already held Vincent Pallotti to be a saint; now I am fully convinced of it."

Men must, according to their natures, struggle for the things they believe in. A week before this blow fell, Vincent had received a note from Cardinal Brignoli, who evidently knew that something was in the wind, and in it he advises Vincent not to allow himself to be excessively afflicted and that the Holy Father should be approached in order to ascertain what was his true opinion of the Society of the Catholic Apostolate and its mission. Vincent's friends rallied around him; documents, memorials and explanations were prepared under his direction and presented in the proper quarters. The cumulative effect of all these efforts was that the Holy Father declared: "I was not informed of all these things," and in consequence the decree of dissolution was held up, and it finally vanished into the limbo where such unexecuted documents go. The Society of the Catholic Apostolate was saved.

The threat had been directed not only against the title of the Society but against the entity itself. It was not a chance blow from the darkness, or an anonymous assault by masked men. It came from within a great agency of the church; its authors, and those who had advised it, were people of reputation and prestige. Pallotti had asked for persecution at the hands of people who lived according to "the spirit of God." Here they were; here was the answer to his prayer for chastisement from the hands of the just.

The question must now be raised of Pallotti's prudence. It had happened before in the history of the Church that good and holy men became possessed of some splendid theoretical plan, which if applied in proper circumstances would go far to solve the problems of suffering humanity. Insulated by a crystal wall from stern reality, impelled into inconsidered courses by some uncontrolled inner spring of action, such people can possess all the virtues save prudence. Was Pallotti one of these, no matter how holy in private life? Had he really thought out what he wanted to do, and had he sought the advice of prudent men?

History provides a prompt answer. After he had obtained the approval of the Roman diocesan authorities and that of the Holy Father for the projected Society and when the membership began to grow, he judged it necessary to publish the aims and methods with which the Society was inspired. After taking this step, he went on to get the opinions of learned and expert men, and for this purpose he addressed himself to one hundred and seven of the most qualified people in Rome: Cardinals, Rectors of ecclesiastical colleges, Superiors and Procurators General of religious orders and congregations, parish priests and others, requesting them to read over the statement of the aims and methods of the Catholic Apostolate and to make such comments as suggested themselves. The consultation was made in writing at intervals during the years 1837 and 1838, and the answers were also given in writing. They are uniformly favorable and in particular we will record the names of the ten Cardinals who were consulted, and whose answers have been preserved. They were Cardinals Lambruschini, Pedicini, Patrizi, Giustiniani, Odescalchi, Galeffi, Falzacappa, Brignoli, Polidori and Del Drago.

All the founders of the religious communities within the Church have been, it may not be doubted, prudent people, whom we would expect to take counsel with the wise regarding their undertaking. But we doubt if many instances can be found, perhaps not even one, in which a founder consults with no less than one hundred and seven people!

Further, Pallotti was very much concerned, as soon as he had founded the Society, with obtaining spiritual favors for its associates, in conformity with the doctrine that grace bestowed by God on an individual may often be the result of the prayers and good works offered to God by other people who need not necessarily be acquainted with the person whom God decides to favor. Religious orders and communities are wont to grant such "spiritual favors," namely, a share in the good deeds and prayers of their members, to individuals and to other societies in the Church. During the years 1836 and 1837, Vincent obtained this communication of "spiritual favors" for the Society of the Catholic Apostolate from thirteen monastic orders, sixteen mendicant orders, eight orders of regular clerks; five religious congregations. Would the superiors of these institutions, among which we find Benedictines, Franciscans, Dominicans, Jesuits, Redemptorists and Passionists, have been so incautious as to extend their "spiritual treasures" to a doubtful or questionable organization?

Finally, we have it from the highest authority, the trees are known by their fruits. We imagine that it must have cost Vincent Pallotti many a sigh to consent to the preparation of a certain document which set forth, in the year 1838, the successes which the Society of the Catholic Apostolate had already to its credit, but the avowal of them had become necessary in face of the allegations which had been made against it. The document supplies us with the entire history of the activities of the Society up to the year 1838, and is therefore a piece of history, and as such, fits completely into our record. Here it is:

"The Society was born among a group of pious people who for many years past have been wont to obtain the names of missionaries being sent abroad under the auspices of Propaganda, and to furnish these missionaries with the largest possible quantities of pictures, books, rosaries and other pious objects. Since its institution the Society has continued this practice, supplying in addition, vestments, chalices, statues, relics for altarstones, etc."

That the missionaries who were assisted in this way were a very large number indeed appears from another paragraph in this document, which states that they were all authorized to recruit Catholics in their respective mission fields for membership in the Society of the Catholic Apostolate. The following countries are mentioned: China, the East and West Indies, America, Korea, Tibet, Persia, Chaldea, Mesopotamia, Syria, Palestine, Egypt, Asia Minor, Greece, Bulgaria, Wallachia, Transylvania, Poland, Switzerland, Germany, Albania, France, Spain, England, Ireland, Scotland, Africa and many of the Italian States.

The document then refers to the night schools, which the Society was helping to support; the hospitals, where sick people were visited by associates; the courses of spiritual exercises whose expenses the Society paid for in a certain monastery; the preachers and confessors which the Society supplied on request to institutions which asked for them; the hundred thousand copies of religious works which it had printed and distributed. Reference is also made to the work which the Society performed during the cholera plague which afflicted Rome in 1837, and to the houses which it had established for the children left homeless on that occasion. To these latter undertakings we shall have occasion to allude later on in our story.

The document concludes with the observation that the Society makes a special point of assisting and reactivating institutions already in existence, and that it is willing to undertake any kind of task to which it may be called.

The result of this statement we already know: "The Sovereign Pontiff had not been informed of all these things." But for some time thenceforwards, one may observe that cautiousness already mentioned in the use of the designation "Society of the Catholic Apostolate" in the subsequent documents addressed to the authorities and in publications, lest the opposition again take heart and make a new attack.

The purposes, the methods and the membership of the Society of the Catholic Apostolate were made quite clear from the beginning, but it was not quite so clear how it was to be governed. The members were linked together by charity, of course, but this virtue does not in itself constitute a juridical link, though the latter has no meaning, and can in fact become an intolerable tyranny, unless it is informed by the greatest of all virtues. "Charity," Vincent declared, "is the essential and substantive element of the Society."

The idea gradually came into the foreground that a central body, which would set in motion and co-ordinate the activities of the members, was necessary. The early documents show that this central body was not conceived as exclusively clerical, laymen could and did share in it at the beginning. In later restatements of this idea, Vincent made it clear that a dedicated body of clergy was necessary in order to compose this central body — dedicated in the sense that they were to live in community, organized after the fashion of a religious congregation. This is the body which in time came to be known as the Congregation of the Catholic Apostolate, as distinct from the "Pious Union of the Catholic Apostolate."

There has been much controversy among the students of Vincent's apostolic plan as to whether this dedicated body of priests and brothers already existed in his mind when he instituted the Pious Society, or whether it was a later development of his thought. And in the supposition that the latter hypothesis is correct, the precise moment when he decided to institute it, is also a subject of discussion. Into these controversies we need not enter at all, beyond making just one quotation from Pallotti's writings, in a document written nine years after the foundation of the Pious Society.

"The Pious Society, as it was instituted, so also is it directed by the Congregation of priests who live in community under a rule, since a Pious Union of persons easily loses its activity and its stability owing to the dispersion of the members, unless there be a congregation of priests, who in unison constitute a state of life in community and perfect common life . . . ."

Among the documents circulated by Vincent for the opinions and criticisms of the chief personages of Rome, there was a draft statute which indicated how the Society was to be governed. This draft established that, in order to provide for order and hierarchy in the Pious Society, it was to be divided into three classes or sections, corresponding to a three-fold division of ministry. One of these is the ecclesiastical ministry; the second consists of the ministry of prayer; the third is made up by those persons who provide material help of whatever nature. Into the first of these sections, secular and regular priests can be admitted and they are not expected to give up any of their previous undertakings. Membership is based upon the free gift of time and priestly service to the work. The work itself is defined as the exercise of the ministry, preaching, administering the sacraments, instructions; the composition and diffusion of good literature; the encouragement of all efforts to receive the faith and enkindle charity. Priests are expected to give their services not only in the church of the Pious Society itself, but also in all other churches where the Society may judge that their assistance is needed. Provision is made that the Society, which can be extended to other dioceses, will be governed by a Central Council, of which the chief officers will be chosen from the members of the first section excepting the treasurer and the bursar, who are to be chosen from among the members of the third section. This draft, which was sent out to a number of people over a period of many months, underwent corrections in the course of the consultations. In one of these corrections an important point emerges. The original draft mentions that the members of the first class acquire no obligation of community life; in the correction it is stated that not *all* the members of this section are bound to community life. From this we draw the conclusion that Vincent, in authorizing this change in the draft, states for the first time that there is to be in the Society a class of members whose incorporation will carry with it the obligation of common life. In another draft, which circulated in the year 1838, this idea of a group of priests who will be permanently associated with the Society is further elaborated. This group will consist of priests who give themselves entirely to the work; they are to be selected after presentation by the Council and they are to do a novitiate of six months, after which date they will be admitted to make a promise of permanence, which is revocable at the will of the parties.

All these factors, taken together, introduce us to Vincent's plan of associating clergy of both orders, prayer groups and laity for a single apostolic purpose: the revival of faith and charity, and the diffusion of these virtues throughout the world. People are to be encouraged to act *in concert* for the good of the Catholic religion. That is why Pius XI, the Pope of Catholic Action, hailed Vincent, when the decree proclaiming the heroicity of his virtues was published, as the Precursor of modern Catholic Action, not only in its substance, but in the name itself.

On the feast of SS. Peter and Paul, in the year 1839, after a hard morning's work in the confessional, Vincent suffered a hemorrhage; on the following day he had another. He consulted a doctor who ordered him to leave Rome as soon as possible. A few days later he went to stay at the Camaldolese Monastery in the hills above Frascati — where he had often stayed before. He intended first to rest and to devote much time to prayer and meditation, and then to undertake two tasks which were urgent. One of these was the drafting of rules of the House of Charity which, with the help of the Pious Society he was supporting in Rome; the second was to write a Rule for the Pious Society of the Catholic Apostolate, which, if adopted, would replace the provisional rules which were being used.

On the 21st of August he wrote as follows to a young priest who was much in his confidence and had just sent him a letter containing a long list of questions and suggestions:

"Yesterday, through God's mercy I finished the rules for the House of Charity.... Today I have commenced to write on the work in general. Tell our Lady to enter into my mind, my heart, my pen. The Queen of the Apostles must do everything.... God in His mercy has given me the grace of knowing the necessity of writing everything, but you must pray, and have others pray, that I be given time and light...."

The young priest had in his letter given his opinion that Vincent was destined to live a long life. Replying to this prediction, Vincent says:

"May God give me that length of life which He wishes, and how He wishes. I feel that in order to lay the bases carefully of all the Rules and set about putting them into execution, many years of life would be necessary for me. But God does not need me. If, in order to use me as an example of His mercy He wishes for me to live as long as St. Romuald, I will receive this gift from His hands through the intercession of Our Lady of Mercies."

In reply to another question whether vows would be introduced as part of the discipline of the priest members of the Association, Vincent goes on to explain what is the state of his mind at that moment regarding the composition of the Pious Society and the links which would bind it together.

"The work is composed of three sections. First, members living in the retreat-houses, colleges, seminaries,

without vows, for the present anyhow; houses of recollection for priests without vows, by means of which the
Society may always be able to unite the secular and regular
clergy for evangelical purposes.... The second section is
composed of women.... The third section is that of the
Associates, who are not joined together in community
life...."

The result of his work at Camaldoli is an 80-page
book (not published during his lifetime) in which
he sets out the principles which should govern the
Society of the Catholic Apostolate in fulfilling its
ministry. It is remarkable for the splendid vision,
truly universal in its breadth, which it lays before us
of the possibilities of the Church in modern times.
There are no national frontiers in this vision. At its
center lies Rome, not the capital of a nation, not even
the inheritor of the ancient culture of the West, but
Catholic Rome, the center of energy of the religion
of Christ. In order to assist Peter's successor in his
perpetual task of interpreting Christianity to the
peoples of the world, and perpetually energizing
the Message which was of old committed to the
Sovereign Pontiff, Pallotti proposes to put in his hand
a new agency, which does not pretend to replace
any existing agency, or existing source of spiritual
energy; which, on the contrary, will act in comity
and charity with them all.

This new agency will be the Society of the Catholic Apostolate, which views the spiritual needs and
the spiritual maladies of the world and seeks to
remedy them according to a due order. Vincent considered that the Society of the Catholic Apostolate
should direct its efforts to a single end, but taking
account of the diversity of the problems. Hence he
divides the activities of the Society of the Catholic
Apostolate into thirteen sections, which he calls
Procures. Each of these Procures is to be dedicated
to an apostle. (The number thirteen is obtained by

adding St. Paul to the Twelve). Each Procure, under its respective apostle, must undertake a specific task.

The first Procure is placed under the patronage of St. Peter, and has for its office, the promotion of the spiritual, scientific and pastoral culture of the clergy.

The second, dedicated to St. Andrew, will promote the work of the missions and spiritual exercises for the people.

The third, under the patronage of the Apostle James, will promote the work of foreign missions among clergy and people.

The fourth, dedicated to St. John, will undertake to develop associations for charitable and religious purposes among the people.

The fifth, under the patronage of the Apostle Thomas, will seek to promote the religious, civil and literary education of youth of both sexes, particularly the poor.

The sixth, dedicated to St. James the Less, will undertake to collect and provide objects suitable for increasing the devotion of the people of God and His saints.

The seventh, under the patronage of St. Philip, will promote the religious and moral interests of rural workers.

The eighth, dedicated to St. Bartholomew, will endeavor to alleviate the lot of all prisoners.

The ninth, under the patronage of St. Matthew, will undertake to assist the sick in their material and spiritual necessities.

The tenth, dedicated to St. Simon, will address itself to the spiritual interests of soldiers and the upper classes of society.

The eleventh, under the patronage of St. Jude Thaddeus, will endeavor to propagate all forms of collective devotion approved by the Church.

The twelfth, dedicated to St. Matthias, will seek to assist orphans, widows, and the friendless poor.

The thirteenth, under the patronage of St. Paul, will assist and supplement all the other Procures in the execution of their missions.

These Procures, according to Vincent's conception, are not clerical organizations; their strength, both numerically and in the order of activity, is to be drawn from the laity. The clergy are to exercise a directive function, to act as assessors of the laity in the apostolic work.

It is, as we have said, a great and wonderful vision: the Church at the service of the people, not as a mere formula, but organically; the Church taking the lead in organizing men to secure their own welfare in the moral sphere. It is the Church meeting the people, mingling with them, organizing them for God. It is the Church acting on the modern man in the whole range of his activities and his interests; the Church taking account of the insistence with which contemporary man demands organization as the surest remedy for his ills.

For any founder to put into execution so vast a plan, as Vincent observed in the letter quoted above, would require a long lifetime, and Providence was not granting him many more years. He, therefore, warned his followers that they must not expect the plan to be fulfilled immediately, and that their efforts must be directed to putting into practice these parts of it which could be most readily applied, taking into account the circumstances of time and place. The activation of the plan was made conditional on its acceptance by the bishops in their dioceses, for Pallotti was nothing if not respectful of proper jurisdiction.

How much of the plan ever did go into execution? Pallotti in his own life certainly performed, not one alone, or just a few, of the tasks laid down in the lineaments of the various Procures; he shared in all of them, from assisting the destitute poor and widows and orphans, to promoting the spiritual, scientific and pastoral culture of the clergy. His followers, now in one country, now in another, now at one time, now at another, have never forgotten his vision of the apostolate and have realized portions of it in various ways. And we may also say that the ideals which God communicated to Pallotti have, whether through his agency or that of other holy souls, gradually made their way into the whole Catholic Church. There is no place in the world today where the Catholic Church does not meet men and exert its influence upon them according to some plan or method of apostolate, which on analysis will be found to be substantially the same as Pallotti's vision.

We must now go back a little in the order of time and refer to another of the surviving memorials of Pallotti's life: his institution of the great popular Octave of the Epiphany in the city of Rome. Few religiously-minded visitors to this city during the Christmas season can fail to have attended it, for it marks the closure of the Christmas celebrations in Rome. It commences on the eve of the Epiphany and closes on the Octave day. There are so many features and elements in it, that it is impossible to single out any one in particular and say that here is the meaning, the essence of the entire celebration. In the first place, it is a feast of the Liturgies, for every morning Mass is chanted in one or other of the great Eastern Liturgies, in which the Holy Sacrifice is offered in those parts of the world – the Byzantine rite, the Syro-Antiochene, the Coptic and so on. There are High Masses as well in the variant Latin rites: the Milanese, the Dominican and the Carmelite. Then there are sermons preached each day in one or other of the principal languages of Europe: English, French, German, Spanish and so on. In the afternoons the celebration takes on the character of a great popular mission, with sermons delivered by some celebrated Italian preacher. The evening services conclude with a solemn procession and Benediction given by a Cardinal each evening, attended by one of the great ecclesiastical colleges of Rome in an order of precedence which was laid down over a century ago. The celebration is held in the largest church in the popular quarter of Rome—that quarter where Vincent Pallotti was born and lived all his life. The streets traversed by the prelates, ecclesiastics and people coming to the service, are the very same streets which he walked in life, hurrying to and fro on his apostolic errands. Many people go to share in the Oriental Liturgies, which are so strange to the Catholics of the West, but Vincent Pallotti did not arrange these services in order to gratify any one's sense of novelty or to satisfy curiosity. He placed them in the Octave because he wanted to show, in dramatic fashion, the universal character of the Catholic religion, which embraces the East and the West, and he wanted the people of the West to pray together with those from the East. These Liturgies, along with the lesser Latin rites, are not mere archaeological and liturgical survivals; they are the Catholic forms of worship of living men and women, all united in one Faith and it is good to show that unity not merely in words but in action as well.

The sermons in the various European languages are much more than compliments to the dignity of the nations whose tongues are used. These sermons were prescribed because this was the traditional season when strangers came to stay in Rome and Vincent was anxious that during their stay they might hear the Gospel in their own languages. The popular mission which goes on in the afternoon has the unequivocal purpose of any other popular mission in the world; the diffusion of the Gospel truths among the people. And the great Cardinalitial procession is designed to make the congregation absorb a visual impression of the glory and dignity which should surround the collective manifestations of religious worship.

At the core of the celebration, which takes place in the presence of an enormous Crib, specially set up in the sanctuary of the church for the occasion, is the Doctrine of the Epiphany, that is, the Christian mission to all the peoples of the earth, symbolized in the Wise Men whom tradition ascribes to different races of people. Pallotti's Octave has therefore a missionary signification.

There is also the idea of unity. The Catholic Church has of old defined just what she understands by this word: one Lord, one Faith, one Baptism. Within this unity, there can be, and are, many diversities, and here, at Pallotti's Octave, the various diversities are proudly shown to be no obstacle in the path of the true unity, but rather, they are the legitimate glories which the various races of men have built for themselves in the course of the ages.

There is, too, the idea of a revival of faith among the believers, and the spreading of charity. Faith is spread and deepened in the souls of men by the communication of the Word; charity grows when the sources of the will are touched by the grace which the Creator offers to the men of goodwill who listen to His eternal message. This is the message which the famous preachers of the octave have for generations delivered from the platform pulpit of the great church. This is also the reason why a profusion of pamphlets, leaflets and objects of devotion are given out during these days: Christian literature in its simplest expression, designed to act directly on the mind and heart.

And finally there is the cooperation between the different religious bodies and the secular clergy which is indispensable for the celebration of the Epiphany on the grand scale in which it has always been carried out. The prelates, the secular clergy, the religious orders, the seminarians and members of the ecclesiastical colleges unite here not only in theory but in complete reality in order to symbolize the deep underlying union which must always exist in God's church between the secular and regular clergy, if God's work in the world is to be done. How these celebrations, made possible only by this co-operation of the clergy, must have rejoiced Pallotti's heart! For that was indeed one of the great ideals on which his mind was set from the beginning of his priestly career right up to the end.

"The celebration of the octave of the Epiphany (Pallotti wrote) not only promotes the propagation of the faith and shows the identity of dogma by means of the diversity of rites, but increases charity among secular and regular ecclesiastics of all rites and religious bodies, who for this purpose are invited to take part in the functions of the octave."

The first celebration of the octave of the Epiphany was organized by Vincent in the year 1836 and it has been celebrated continuously ever since, with two exceptions: one in 1849, when the occupation of Rome by the revolutionaries made it inexpedient; and another in 1871 when an inundation of the Tiber flooded the quarter of Rome where the octave is celebrated. The celebrations have nearly always taken place at the great church of St. Andrea della Valle, save on a few occasions when repairs to the church or other incidental reasons made it advisable to use another church for the purpose.

Vincent's surviving correspondence shows what a great deal of effort and activity he employed in the annual organization of the celebration. Not only was it necessary to visit and invite the prelates for the ceremonies as well as the rectors of colleges and the other personages involved; transport must be provided in many cases. He used to resort to his friends among the Roman nobility for the loan of their carriages for this purpose; and he asked for their monetary contributions for the same end. The great crib was donated by the famous Torlonia family.

The Epiphany celebration keeps Vincent's name green in his native Rome, as it keeps his ideals before the minds of those who seek to penetrate the inner meaning of the great festival.

We will go on now to deal with two further undertakings of Vincent which have also stood the test of time—the House of Charity and the Conservatory of the Sacred Heart. The origin of these establishments is linked historically with the great cholera plague which laid Rome waste in the year 1837. This desperate malady made its appearance in Europe in the year 1830, when it appeared in Moscow, spread into Poland, Austria, England and France, reaching Marseilles in 1835, where it created terrible havoc. The inhabitants of all Europe were terrified as each spring and summer came round, dreading where it would appear next. The origin and causes of contagion were unknown and the precaution chiefly resorted to was that of the sanitary cordon. Nevertheless, Gregory XVI already in 1831 drew up a series of measures about the public sanitation and furthermore sent a commission of three doctors to Paris in order to study the course of the malady and determine which means were best to employ in preventing and curing it. In 1835 the cholera appeared in the north of Italy, laid Venice waste and attacked Leghorn and Florence. A year later it appeared in Naples. Finally that same year, the malady showed up in Ancona, which was part of the papal states.

The Roman spring of 1837 was not indeed a good season; an extraordinary number of cases of grippe or influenza appeared and the people of the city lived in fear of what the next summer might bring. That same spring Naples was stricken by cholera once more. In July it showed up in some of the towns and villages near Rome and the city was in terror. At the end of that month three doubtful cases were taken into one of the city hospitals and the city filled with rumors. Denials were published at first, but in the end the truth was known. Cholera was in the city. The mortality index began to climb; those who could, fled; those who were forced to stay, looked with dread into each other's faces, seeking the first symptoms which empiric knowledge associated with the appearance of the disease. People were by decree forbidden to assemble in numbers; factories with more than a small number of workmen were closed and police powers were extended.

The cholera death-rate, a dreadful thermometer, commenced at the end of July with one case; by the end of August the highest mark was reached, five hundred and seventeen deaths in one day. After that the rate declined, and by October it had disappeared, leaving behind it a trail of disrupted and broken homes, fatherless children, sorrow and enmities. Almost ten percent of the population had been affected by the disease.

His biographer Melia, who stood by Vincent's side all through the emergency, records that the latter was literally besieged in his confessional all day long and a great part of the night by people anxious to make their peace with God before it was too late. The only interruption he permitted himself was to attend the sick-calls which grew ever more numerous as the death-rate increased. Vincent was himself quite fearless and remained with the sick as long as was necessary, without showing any desire for precipitate withdrawal. There came a moment when he himself was attacked by what were generally regarded as early symptoms of the disease. He must have thought it was upon him, for he called Melia and showed him where certain effects were stored, and instructed him what to do with them in the case of death.

Vincent's compassion for the stricken was made manifest whenever he was called upon to attend the sufferers.

"Vincent (writes Melia) acted towards them like a mother solicitous for her dear children; he administered medicines to them, gave them to drink, adjusted their beds, raised them up when required, gave them courage to bear everything with patience for the sake of God, consoled them in the most affectionate manner, in a word tried to afford them every possible corporal relief."

The plague swiftly created a social problem. The dependents of the sick and the dead had to be fed; there were no wages for the workingmen and the artisans who had been laid off for fear of contagion. People fled from the plague-houses and roamed the streets, homeless and without food, bedding and proper clothing. There was, it is true, public relief, but the magnitude of the disaster had overwhelmed all previsions. Vincent immediately directed the Society of the Catholic Apostolate to grapple with the problem, and in the intervals which he could snatch from the confessional and the sick beds, a plan was drawn up and carried out.

"The Society of the Catholic Apostolate placed at the door of the sacristy of the church a box, to which everybody had access. They merely had to state their names, addresses and parish on a piece of paper and later the members of the Society, two by two, visited the addresses and left with them coupons for bread and meat and lemons (which were considered a specific against the cholera); others were supplied with clothing and beds; others who had pawned their goods had the pledges redeemed; workingmen without work were paid for work to be performed in the future. The priests of the Society attended the sick day and night."

A coupon system was created and proved very successful. The Society aided those parishes where no organization had been set up by supplying them with coupons so that they too could take care of their ailing poor. A year after the cessation of the cholera outbreak, the Society was still distributing coupons to the needy.

The major social problem which the cholera left in its wake was the large number of orphan children, who, bereft of one or both parents, wandered through the streets begging. Some of them, no doubt, had no one to turn to; others were forced by cruel relatives to resort to this extremity.

The problem had existed in Rome before the cholera, which merely aggravated it. Vincent had already directed the attention of the Society of the Catholic Apostolate to it shortly after its foundation, and it was decided, even before the epidemic, to create some kind of home where girls especially might be housed, fed and educated. Vincent had it in mind as well that the Society should develop as soon as possible a community of religious women under its own direction. At this time he was also thinking much about the missionary college he planned to establish and he felt that if a community of pious women could be created, the missionary project would also benefit from it.

In the beginning the Society tried to cope with the problem of the mendicant children by first placing them here and there among the associates themselves. A house was then rented near the church of St. Mary Major; the children were collected there and handed over to a group of trustworthy women who secured assistance from other sources as well as the Society. Then they took over all the responsibility and continued with the work on their own account. But fresh cases kept cropping up and in order to take care of them the Society then made an arrangement with a lady who for years had been keeping a number of children first in her home, and later in a building put at her disposal by a charitable society. The Society of the Catholic Apostolate paid her a fixed sum for boarding as many children as were sent to her. But the lady passed away and most of these children were then taken over by Giacomo Salvati who figures earlier in our story—and lodged temporarily in a house he possessed.

Then came the cholera and its aftermath. It became urgently necessary to obtain ampler premises to house the fatherless children. After some time a large building, formerly an ecclesiastical college, was secured. This took place in March 1838 and the girls were shortly afterward transferred to the new establishment. The domestic direction of the House of Charity was at first given into the hands of a group of teachers, and the Society kept charge of the spiritual and financial aspects of the undertaking.

The inmates of the House were taught the usual school subjects and also spinning, dressmaking or other useful trades, and when they arrived at a convenient age, places were found for them in the world. About seventy girls could be lodged in the institution.

At the end of the year 1840 the Society of the Catholic Apostolate was offered the opportunity of purchasing a large house in another part of Rome, which appeared suitable for extending the work of the House of Charity. With the assistance of several benefactors the deal was concluded and the lady who had hitherto been in charge of the House of Charity, with part of the staff and a proportion of the inmates, removed to this house, which was dedicated to the Sacred Heart. The new house was conducted under the same rules as the House of Charity, and the Society continued to provide spiritual and material assistance to the community. Shortly afterward the Torlonia family became interested in this second charitable establishment and took over the responsibility for the administration.

In the year 1841 Dr. Russell, President of Maynooth College in Ireland, was in Rome and he paid this tribute to the Pallotti homes in a letter to a friend in Ireland:

"The Abbate Pallotti has established since the cholera, plain houses throughout the entire city and has already provided for a prodigious number of the helpless creatures. I said Mass in one of them the other day and nothing could exceed the order, comfort and contentment which pervaded it."

Vincent's desire that the original House of Charity should be placed in the hands of a community of religious organized by the Society for this purpose was not immediately carried out, though the lady in charge, as we learn from an account of the transfer of the establishment from Salvati's house to the new building, was already wearing religious garb. This, it would appear, was an act of devotion on her part. Several years were in fact to pass before the religious life, according to the rule of the Society of the Catholic Apostolate, was at last organized; the first sister to become a member of this new branch of the Apostolate, received the habit on March 30, 1843. The seedling sown that day has grown into a strong tree, with roots firmly planted in many countries. Vincent's aspiration that the Society of the Catholic Apostolate should also be developed as a community among women consecrated to the religious life was first carried out in the way we have related, but it is not the only way in which Providence was to fulfill that aspiration reserved for it. Several other communities of women have at various times been organized, in accordance with the original idea, in various parts of the world, under their own superiors and with the steady assistance of the priests of the Society. These communities, off-shoots from a common root are doing their share in carrying out the Pallottian ideal of reviving faith and spreading charity throughout the world.

Just before he died, Vincent was preparing to establish another House of Charity in the town of Velletri, some miles from Rome. A gentleman living in that place became acquainted with the House of Charity in Rome and, admiring its rules and the spirit which animated it, invited Vincent to make a foundation in his native town. A house and site was purchased, permission from the ecclesiastical superiors was obtained, but before the building was ready for occupation, Vincent had gone to his glory. The Velletri house, which was opened finally in 1852 still remains in the hands of the Sisters of the Catholic Apostolate and continues to serve faithfully the ideals for which it was founded.

Some of the sisterhoods which form part of the Society of the Catholic Apostolate are bound together by voices; others, like the priests and brothers of the Society have promises as the element of their stability; some are religious communities in the traditional sense of the word; others belong rather to the class of secular institutes. The bond of unity between them all is fidelity to Pallotti and his apostolic aspirations.

Vincent lays down very clearly in the document dated 1838, what were the chief activities in which the priest-members of the Society were to engage.

"The works proper to the Society are: the apostolic ministry, preaching, instructing, administering the sacraments and encouraging people to receive them frequently, the curbing of vice and error, the propagation of the spirit of religion and piety; the composition and publication of books for the purpose of explaining, defending and maintaining religion; the encouragement and propagation of devotions and religious practices which tend to awaken faith, increase piety and correct evil; the performance of the ecclesiastical ministry not only in the churches of the Society but in other churches and places where services are asked for."

These various enterprises are concerned with the spiritual benefit of the populations of the Catholic countries. But Vincent wanted his Society to interest itself in the whole world, and consequently he goes on to describe what the Society should do for the foreign missions:

"As regards those countries which are pagan or heterodox in their religion, the Society will perform the following tasks: assist in the training of the hearts and minds of those called to the foreign missions, seek to increase vocations for the missions...get in touch with missionaries in the field and learn what their needs are...; help the Propaganda in Rome...; produce books on religion in the languages of these countries which lack such books...; gather information on the missions and publish it...; secure the interest and assistance of the bishops and other influential persons for the missions...."

These are the tasks which the members of the Society have been doing from the beginning; they are the tasks which are being done today wherever the spiritual children of Vincent Pallotti are working for God's kingdom on earth.

CHAPTER V

The Universal Apostolate

Because of his solicitude for the training of the future clergy in Rome, Vincent became widely known to the superiors of the colleges where this training was being imparted. The chief places where he carried out this apostolate were the Roman Seminary and the Propaganda College, in both of which he was for many years, as we noticed earlier, the spiritual director. In both establishments there were students from the English-speaking lands, destined to become famous prelates in later days. Let us briefly glance at the careers of some of them and observe how their youthful contact with the burning priestly zeal of Pallotti affected the course of their lives. There was, for instance, Tobias Kirby, a native of Tullow, in Waterford, Ireland, who came to Rome in the year 1829, aged twenty-five years, with the intention of studying theology. While he was yet undecided in which college to enroll, he spent a short holiday in Subiaco, and a fellow guest in the house where he was staying happened to be the famous Scripture scholar, John Allemand, who was a spiritual disciple of Pallotti. On the advice of this professor, Kirby enrolled in the Roman Seminary and thus commenced his long association with Vincent, who became his spiritual director. Kirby remained in Rome after his ordination.

"I continued to frequent Vincent's company (he deposed in the Process), either by taking part in the conferences for ecclesiastics which he conducted at his church or by sharing in his pious undertakings as an external cooperator. I attained great familiarity with him.... In the Roman Seminary we all thought he was a saint...."

He was appointed Vice-Rector of the Irish College and his veneration for Pallotti led him to secure his services for the spiritual instructions of the students and for retreats and conferences. Vincent was Kirby's guest at the college during the dark days of 1849, at the time when Pallotti's life was in danger from the revolutionaries. A year later Kirby became Rector of the college and held the post during nearly forty years, but did not limit himself exclusively to his rectorial duties, for he continued to attend sick people in hospitals, to take part in charitable associations, to help out other priests in their engagements. That is to say, he continued to live as Pallotti would have wished. After his death this tribute was paid to him in a commemorative speech:

"Tobias Kirby lived always under the vivid impression of Pallotti's heroic virtue, and he gave himself with extraordinary energy to the apostolate. He had a special predilection for assisting the dying. Once he contracted the plague and almost died, but after his recovery he returned once more to the same slum in order to resume the same work. It was his favorite apostolate."

In his old age Kirby was appointed Archbishop of Ephesus by Pope Leo XIII who had been his classmate in the Roman University. He has left to posterity a manual of meditations for clergy which is deeply impregnated with the Pallottian spirituality.

Another Irishman who knew and venerated Pallotti at the Roman Seminary was Bartholomew Woodlock, who was later to be Rector of Newman's University in Dublin, and Bishop of Ardagh and Clonmacnoise in Ireland. Woodlock came to Rome in 1836, entered the Roman Seminary and stayed in it till his graduation in 1842.

"I had a very high opinion of Vincent Pallotti (he declared) and his reputation among the students was that of a saint. There was talk of a bilocation and that he slept only two hours every night."

Woodlock recalled, forty years later, that Pallotti sometimes used to hear the confessions of the students in the Roman College, in a standing or kneeling position, because, in Woodlock's opinion, he was resisting a tendency to sleep. He also related that in the intervals between confessions, Pallotti used to change his posture by kneeling down, for the same reason. Woodlock became ill during his course and was advised to return home, and in his indecision, applied to Pallotti to know what to do; he was advised by Vincent to stay and complete his course, which he did without prejudice to his health.

"I am devoted to Vincent Pallotti (Woodlock stated in the Process) because he introduced me to the ecclesiastical life and gave me much excellent spiritual advice."

John Spalding, later Archbishop of Baltimore, was a student of the Propaganda College from the years 1830 to 1834. Reflecting on the formative influences of his youth in that great establishment, he made this statement many years afterwards to a priest of the Society of the Catholic Apostolate:

"Vincent Pallotti was well known to all Rome for his eminent sanctity. We well remember him as we knew him forty years ago, when we gloried in the honor of his spiritual direction. The good odor of his virtues still sweetens our memory and like a halo clusters round our heart. What impressed us as the most striking traits in Vincent's character were his mortification, including the entire forgetfulness of self, his unflagging charity to all, especially towards his penitents; his patience which no disappointment or cross could ruffle; his deep humility which made him consider himself the last of men; his relentless zeal, which continually burned in his heart with a subdued and steady flame; and finally and above all his ardent love of God and of Jesus Christ in His sacred humanity as well as in His divinity. This love which prompted and was the life and soul of all his actions was at the same time the key to his wonderful equanimity and the source of all his fortitude. In addition it provided the wellspring of an internal peace which beamed outwardly, heaven-like in his countenance.

"For almost forty years of missionary life Vincent's benign and saintly face has continued to beam upon us, directing, guiding, teaching us with a divine sternness and compassion. Thus we cannot find it in our hearts to stray far or long from the straight path which he carved out so impressively by his instructions and more eloquently by his example. To follow both more faithfully would further advance us on the way of perfection."

We have already told how Wiseman, on the eve of his episcopal consecration, consulted Pallotti and received momentous counsel from him. They were known to each other long before this event, for Pallotti often visited the English College and highly esteemed Wiseman's great gifts. When he sought the opinions of theologians regarding the foundation of the Society Wiseman was one of those whose counsel was asked for. It was given in the following terms, on January 17, 1837.

"I have read attentively the plan and rules of 'The Catholic Apostolate' of Rome and I approve of it completely, and I welcome its propagation and perfect success, for the glory of God and the salvation of souls."

Wiseman's interest in Pallotti's foundation induced him, on one occasion, to make an unusual suggestion: that Pallotti should approach John Henry Newman, in 1847, who was preparing for the priesthood in Rome, and recruit him for the Society of the Catholic Apostolate! So we learn from a letter written to Vincent by Fr. Melia who was at that time a missionary in London and was in close touch with Bishop Wiseman in that city.

"Monsignor Wiseman (Melia wrote) has told me that he wishes you to speak to Mr. Newman at the Propaganda, who has not yet decided which religious institution he will join; he may perhaps prefer to join the Catholic Apostolate, were its nature and importance explained to him."

We do not know if Vincent took any steps in this direction. It was not his practice to seek out candidates for his community; he relied on Providence to send him such collaborators as were necessary.

At the time of the Vatican Council, many of the English-speaking prelates present were alumni of the Propaganda and the Irish College, who recollected Pallotti from their student days and rejoiced to hear that the cause of his beatification was under consideration. In order to speed it up and to add the testimony of their gratitude they signed Postulatory Letters to the Holy See. The list of their names and styles reads like the roll-call of advancing Catholicism in the English-speaking world: James Quin, Bishop of Brisbane in Australia; Timothy O'Mahony, Bishop of Armidale in Australia and later of Toronto, Canada; Daniel Murphy, formerly Vicar-Apostolic of Nagpur and then Archbishop of Hobart, Tasmania; Thomas Power, Bishop of St. John's, Newfoundland; Thomas Croke, Vicar-Apostolic of Auckland and later Archbishop of Cashel, in Ireland; Henry Elder, Bishop of Natchez and later Archbishop of Cincinnati; Patrick Moran, Bishop of Ossory in Ireland and later Cardinal Archbishop of Sydney in Australia. To these was added at a later date the illustrious name of John Henry Cardinal Newman, who became acquainted with Pallotti during his stay in Rome in the years 1846-47.

Cardinal Acton, of the Anglo-Italian family of that name, who was one of the Curial Cardinals in Rome till his death in 1847, gave his trust and friendship to Pallotti during that period. From Pallotti's correspondence we learn that he used on occasion to send poor people in need of alms to the Cardinal, with whom that recommendation was enough to enlist his ready generosity. The Cardinal was one of the early patrons of the Society of the Catholic Apostolate and his name was set down as one of those who were prepared to receive donations for it.

Another undertaking dear to Vincent's heart was the weekly Conference for Ecclesiastics, which was created for the secular and the regular clergy, for the discussion of practical matters of the apostolate, for prayer in common and lectures from competent ecclesiastics on some point of discipline. These conferences were first held in the Church of the Holy Spirit and developed from the recitation in common of the Devout Exercises of the Month of Mary for Ecclesiastics, according to the method outlined by Vincent in the Manual he prepared for that purpose. When the seat of the Society was transferred to San Salvatore, the conferences were held there and were continued for many years, right up to the present century. Informal, quiet and unpublicized reunions, these conferences contributed to the growth of brotherly feelings among the clergy, to their piety and their greater efficiency in dealing with the problems of the priesthood in the world.

During the summer of 1840 Vincent suffered another severe breakdown in health and was obliged to leave Rome for several months. The crisis in the affairs of his beloved Catholic Apostolate, which had appeared so menacing two years earlier, was for the moment quiescent. The Society under his leadership had succeeded with two of its enterprises: the octave of the Epiphany and the foundation of the Houses of Charity; but it had so far proved impossible to set up the central house which had been deemed necessary; the project of the foreign missionary college was meeting with difficulties; prudence advised that incorporation of new members should be done quietly and that little publicity should be

given to the title of the Society. The powerful opposition had not disappeared; at any moment, stimulated by any capricious incident, it might break into
activity again and the second onslaught might prove
fatal to the Pallottian *opus.* Vincent retired to rest
and recuperate, first at Cingoli and then at Osimo
in the Marches. He was pursued into these quiet
retreats by numerous correspondents, but time was
available for him to look into the recesses of his
soul and to scrutinize the future with a tranquility
which in Rome was never easily available and had
to be obtained at the expense of rest and sleep. He
has left two remarkable documents from this period
which help us to understand the man and the inner
peace which never left him even in the busiest and
most hectic moments. One of these documents is
incorporated in his Spiritual Diary.

"On October 10, 1840, during recollection after Holy
Mass, our blessed Lord gave me to understand how in the
most Blessed Sacrament of the Eucharist He is my food
and nourishment; not only by the communication of His
sanctity and perfection, but also by the communication
of His own life and fortitude and by providing me with
strength to live with all reasonable serenity, for His greater
glory and the advantage of souls, according to His most
admirable and holy will. This feeling has led me into a
more peaceful security that whatever is or will be the state
of my bodily health, everything will be according to what
His mercy and not His justice wishes. O my God, my sins
have merited death and eternal condemnation, but You
grant me life, when and how You will it, through Your
mercy and the merits of our Lord and our blessed Lady
and the saints."

During this same period of grave illness at
Osimo, when Vincent was so much alone with his
own soul and away from most of the daily distractions
of an active life, he records in his Diary a second profound spiritual experience. The document shows that
at this time he submerged himself in the contempla-

tion of the tremendous Eucharistic mystery of God becoming the food of men's souls. He first dwells on the august Trinitarian mystery:

"By the eternal and infinite contemplation of Himself, God engenders the Son, who is the living and perfect Image of the substance of God Himself. I am infinitely unworthy and incapable of being like unto God; nevertheless He nourishes me with the living Image of His divine substance, and this food destroys all my unworthiness, past, present and future...and God Himself is within me, abides in me, works in me.

"Because of their eternal and infinite resemblance, the Father and the Son love one another with an eternal and infinite love, and in this is the very love with which God infinitely and eternally loves Himself. God deigns to nourish me most mercifully with His infinite and eternal love...and by means of it, destroys in me all my unworthiness, destroys in me all profane and earthly love and makes the love of God live, abide and operate in me."

The Eucharistic food which men receive in Holy Communion is not circumscribed to the material body of Christ, for Christ is God and it is the total Christ—body, blood, soul and divinity—who nourishes the soul of man. At this stage of his contemplation Vincent turns his thoughts to the majestic divine attributes which so fascinated him in the first stages of his spiritual life and he then goes on to explain to himself how these attributes play their part in the nourishment of his soul.

"God is infinite and eternal Power, infinitely merciful, and I am infinitely weak and infinitely unworthy of the gifts of God...nevertheless He nourishes me infinitely and eternally with His infinite and eternal power and destroys in me all my weakness, in such fashion that this very weakness will not prejudice my poor soul and its efforts for the glory of God and the advantage of souls which God demands of me.

"God is eternal wisdom and I am infinitely unworthy of light from God and the influence of His wisdom...but by His nourishment He destroys my unworthiness and the evil effects of my culpable ignorance, and I firmly believe as well that He destroys the very darkness of my ignorance.

"God is infinite, eternal and essential love, and although I am infinitely unworthy to possess in my heart the outpouring of divine charity...this nourishment destroys in my heart all profane and earthly love.

"God is essential justice, and although I have been unjust to God, to my fellowman and myself...in the Holy Eucharist God nourishes me with His justice, and destroys in me all my injustice....

"God is infinite and essential purity, and I am essentially impure. In the Eucharist He nourishes me with His own infinite purity and destroys all my impurity and all its consequences; and this destruction once accomplished, God Himself, who is infinite, essential, eternal, immense and infinitely merciful purity, lives in me....

"God is infinite, essential and eternal mercy and I am essentially cruel and gross. In the Eucharist He nourishes me with His very own mercy and destroys all crudity and grossness, and this destruction once accomplished, the infinitely merciful God abides in me....

"God is eternal; He nourishes me with His eternity in the Eucharist and destroys in me the guilt of all the time I have frittered away, and particularly the time employed in offending Him....

"God is immense; He nourishes me with His incomprehensible immensity and destroys all my pettiness and narrowness, and this destruction once accomplished, His immensity works within me...for His greater glory and the sanctification of souls....

"The sanctity of God is infinite, eternal, essential, immense and incomprehensible; in the Eucharist He nourishes me with His own eternal sanctity and destroys all my evil, and this destruction, once accomplished, the infinite sanctity of God abides in me; I have no sanctity of my own, but it is God's sanctity in me which absorbs me completely and destroys me utterly and God abides in me. What a wonderful invention of divine love!...

"The perfection of God is infinite, eternal, immense, essential and incomprehensible. In the Eucharist He nourishes me with His own infinite perfection and destroys my innumerable imperfections, and this destruction once accomplished, God in His infinite perfection abides in me; it is not my perfection, but the perfection of God in me. O incomprehensible mercy! O infinite love with which I have never corresponded, which I have never loved!..."

The reader will have observed the constant repetition of the word "destruction" in these extracts. This is an important word in the Pallottian spirituality and it is essentially linked with the doctrine, held with great firmness from the beginning of his spiritual life, that vice is to be overcome and destroyed by the cultivation of the opposite and contrary virtue, and that the source of all virtue in man lies in the imitation of our Lord. This great doctrine was symbolized in the formula: *Ad Destruendum Peccatum* — for the destruction of sin — which he always placed at the head of all his correspondence, usually in the form of the initials ADP.

The spiritual illuminations which God had granted to Vincent on this occasion were bound up, not only with his own spiritual life, but also with the work which Providence had specially laid on his shoulders, namely the propagation of the Catholic Apostolate.

In yet another document which he drew up at this time, in the anticipation of an early death, and left to be read by his collaborators after his passage to eternity — as in fact it was so read, for it was discovered among his papers — he gives expression to the idea that the Society was to follow, in its span of existence, the mystic path traced by our Redeemer:

"In order that the Society should be proved in the crucible of tribulation, our Lord permitted that the early explanations of its purposes should have been rendered all too briefly. There have therefore been some people, who, not clearly understanding its nature, its purpose and its works, have persecuted it, to the extent that it showed signs of dying. This was necessary so that the Society might bear within itself the image of our crucified Lord. But at the very

moment when it seemed utterly extinguished it gave indica-
tions of renewed life, as happens with the work of God."

The central body of the Society was not yet
constituted in a formal way at this period. The document goes on to recommend to his followers the manner in which they must provide, in case of death, for
the continued existence of the Society. The necessities of the time in which they are living, he reminds
his disciplies, are: the revival of the spirit of faith
and true charity, the cultivation of Christian morals,
a true social order integrated with fraternal Christian affection and proper subordination to authority.
It is the priests of the Catholic Church, both secular
and regular, who must secure these values for the
people; the final justification for the existence of
the Society lies precisely in how it strives to inspire
the clergy to perform that function. The other apostolic works of the Society are important, but they
are as means to an end. In other words, the Society
is not just another apostolic effort; its action in the
last resort must be sacerdotal.

The characteristics which the Society of the
Catholic Apostolate must possess, in accordance
with the mind of its founder, have been emerging
one by one. It was to be an apostolic society; a Marian
society; a society founded on community life; and now
he insists on the conception that it is a sacerdotal
society. The remaining years of Vincent's life were
dedicated in great part to the development of this
final characteristic of his society.

On his return to Rome towards the end of this
year (1840) the care of his various undertakings
once more absorbed him — the two charitable institutes for whose spiritual welfare, and in the case
of the House of Charity, the temporal welfare as
well — he had made himself responsible; the Octave
of the Epiphany whose proper organization depended
so much on his personal efforts; the frequent calls

to monasteries in order to give spiritual counsel to souls on the road of perfection; his confessional which was always crowded with penitents; the abundant correspondence; the visitors who sought advice, recommendations of all sorts, or alms; the calls to attend the sick and the dying; preaching engagements; and at night, the patient writing and rewriting of his apostolic plans and projects; the long vigils in prayer.

The project nearest to his heart now was the consolidation of a community of priests which would carry on the various works of the Catholic Apostolate already in being and according to circumstances put into practice the great plan of apostolate which he had drafted in the hermitage of the Camaldolese monks. He was of course the heart and soul of the community, though he would be the first to disclaim any such attribution; he was faithfully seconded by his old friend and disciple, Raphael Melia, who came to live in the apartment of the Church of the Holy Spirit in the month of August 1837, where Pallotti himself joined him a month after the death of his father. From time to time other priests and some clerical students came and stayed at the Holy Spirit apartment; some of them preparing for missionary life, others because they wanted to cooperate in the priestly work which Vincent and his companions were doing. They came, they learned, and they went. Among them was an Irishman, Henry O'Farrell, who stayed almost two years, returned to his native land and died at the end of the century, parish priest in his native diocese of Limerick; Theodore Noethen, a German who stayed a year and then set off for the American missions, and many others whose names are omitted for the sake of brevity. But the inner core of the community was made up by Pallotti and Melia until another priest joined them in 1842, and the following year, the first brother.

With the assistance of these priests and the others who lived with them for varying periods of time, Pallotti was enabled to carry on and extend the apostolic work in which he was engaged. There were also several priests in the city, religious and secular, who in accordance with the original plan of the Society gave up part of their time to Vincent, who found plenty of occupation for them all.

Gregory XVI, who reigned from 1831 to 1846, was compelled by his foreign policy and by domestic threats of revolution, to maintain a large standing army. To meet the needs of the garrison of Rome he commissioned the Order of the Knights of Jerusalem to establish a military hospital in the city and granted them in 1841 a large building, which had formerly been a hostel for priests, situated in the neighborhood of the church of the Holy Spirit and just across the road from the little church which was later to pass into the hands of the Society. This military hospital was a large establishment, with a daily average of two hundred and fifty patients. Towards the end of 1843 the authorities of the Knights of Jerusalem asked Vincent to take charge of the spiritual ministrations to these sick soldiers, which he promptly did. The Tenth Procure in his great apostolic plan, dedicated to St. Simon the apostle, was designed to serve the spiritual interests of soldiers, and here at last was an opportunity of putting it into execution.

Vincent had a soft spot in his heart for soldiers, men who live under discipline which is not of their own contriving. He realized very clearly the special temptations to which they are subjected: idleness, gambling, drunkenness, impurity, blasphemy. And above all he realized the anguishes of the sick soldier, separated from his family, involved in an impersonal administrative machine. "Much charity," he said, "must be offered them, particularly when they are

sick, or in prison." For he understood very clearly
the difference between ordinary crime and military
crime.

The Knights of Jerusalem were unable to bear
the financial burden of the Military Hospital and
in October 1844 the patients, excepting those who
could not be moved, were transferred to a special
pavillion in the ancient hospital of the Holy Spirit
in Sassia, a title which recalls the days when Saxon
pilgrims used this place as a hostel. Pope Gregory
himself gave orders that Pallotti and his collaborators
were to continue to look after the sick soldiers in
the new location, an order which was accepted with
alacrity. The soldiers who had been left behind when
the transfer was made, were likewise looked after
by the Society.

It was a rewarding apostolate. Vincent considered it of such importance that he wrote a special
rule for all those who took part in it. In this rule
he entered at length into the problems which or-
dinarily arise in such situations: how to deal with
the staff; how to find helpers and auxiliaries, and what
their disposition should be; the spirit in which patients should be treated; the religious aspect of the
hospital rules; relations with secular and regular
clergy who had duties to perform in the hospital;
religious services, communions and retreats for
soldiers; how to induce them to frequent the sacraments; the religious objects which should be placed
in the wards. It is in fact a complete code of procedure destined to reassure and tranquilize the
sick soldier of that day and age, who was not a con-
script but an enrolled man who had very often fled
from his native place and now found himself sick,
homeless and alone in the grip of a vast administrative machine, which was quite impersonal and heed-
less of all individual terrors. They were more familiar
with priests than doctors, these sons of villagers in
remote places, and it fell to the priests to soothe

their fears, dispose them for death if come it must, write their letters, for many of them were illiterate, and supply them with money to supplement the hospital rations. No wonder Vincent found it necessary to organize a group of collaborators and helpers! But it was fruitful work, in which his soul delighted.

The sick soldiers who recovered went back to their barracks and spoke of this fine priest and his assistants and presently Vincent, as his letters show, was called here and there to give sermons and spiritual exercises to groups of soldiers in the barracks. He induced them to celebrate in communal fashion the month of Mary and arranged for special preachers to attend on such occasions.

Vincent and his Society of the Catholic Apostolate continued to attend the troops in the Holy Spirit Hospital till these forces were disbanded at the time of the Roman Revolution in 1849; the hospital was then occupied by the wounded French prisoners among the Papal troops who had stood by their oath. Vincent and his priests kept on attending them till the revolutionaries, after first endeavoring to drive them out by making odious restrictions, finally ordered them to come no more. As Vincent left the building, the glowering revolutionaries and the bewildered French prisoners heard him intone the Te Deum.

In the course of his dealings with soldiers Vincent was often saddened by the profanity and obscenity of language of these soldiers of the Pope. He maintained that the example should come from the officers themselves and suggested that in the Daily Orders an exhortation against blasphemy and obscenity should be included. Then if any officer should chance to hear a soldier blaspheming or uttering an indecency, that officer would be in a position to reprove him. "The reproof however must not be administered with fury but with military bearing, mingled with charity and a proper and proportionate humility!"

He further suggested that the military chaplains in the Pontifical Army should organize a League against blasphemy and obscenity and he went to the trouble of drawing up for them a statute providing for the foundation and the work of such a league.

There is another fact in connection with this work in the military barracks which should endear Vincent's name to all soldiers and to all who mourn their beloved who have died under arms, far from home and alone. This was an association to accompany the dead soldiers of the military hospital to their last resting-place and have collective prayers said for the repose of their souls.

He engaged too in another, very difficult, apostolate. Capital punishment still existed in the Papal States at this time, though the actual number of people executed was in reality very small — an average of two or three per year in the city of Rome. There was an ancient institution, the Confraternity of St. John the Beheaded, whose purpose was to assist the condemned man in his last hours, comfort him and secure for him all the rites of the Church. The Confraternity had its regular chaplain, but in the difficult cases, where despair took possession of the unhappy victim of the rigors of the law, recourse was often made to Pallotti, who on such occasions would sometimes spend the entire night in the condemned man's cell before the execution. His humility, his unction and the grace of his words succeeded in softening the hardest hearts and in bringing comfort to the most desperate souls. He was in time offered the chaplaincy of the Confraternity, which he declined, preferring to give his services on a voluntary basis and not as a fixed obligation.

In the month of August of the year 1844 an act of grace on the part of the Holy Father put an end to the prolonged discomfort and sporadic persecution which Pallotti and his guests and companions had been putting up with at the church of the Holy Spirit.

Vincent was notified that his Society had been granted the ancient little church of San Salvatore, nearby the famous Ponte Sisto. Included in the gift was a fairly large house. This had been in former times the property of the Conventual Franciscan Order and had served for centuries as the residence of the Procurator-General. For some time the church and house had been little used and were presently in bad repair. This grant was a great mercy. No sooner had the house been put into some sort of order than several priests and brothers joined the Society and went to live in San Salvatore.

This was a great joy to Vincent, all the more acceptable because it came after a natural sorrow. His earliest and most faithful companion, Raphael Melia, whom he had known since Melia was a boy, had for some time been urging on Vincent his desire to become a missionary. His thoughts were fixed on England and already in 1839 he had, with Pallotti's permission, taken up the study of the English language. Melia was, in as far as such terms can be applied to ecclesiastics, a man with a career before him; he had been Vice-Rector of the great Propaganda College until its administration was handed back to the Jesuit Fathers; then he was given a post of trust in the Congregation of Propaganda itself; these were responsibilities which in time would be followed by rewards. He had joined Pallotti in his enterprises in early life and had lived continuously with him for several years while continuing to do his work at Propaganda.

In 1843 an Italian priest who lived in London and was chaplain to the Italians resident in that city passed through Rome and informed the Propaganda that he was soon resigning this chaplaincy and that in consequence another priest should be sent there. Fr. Melia, with Pallotti's permission, applied for this post and was granted it.

It was a missionary assignment charged with difficulties. The London Italians were poor and unwelcome among the general population; they had no church of their own, no rallying center. Their religion was under attack from two angles: the sectarians who wanted to convert them to Protestantism, and gave Gospel Teas and such-like entertainments to raise funds in order to pay proselytizing apostates; and the Italian political fuorusciti, mostly anti-clericals who wanted to get their own back on the Pope and the bishops of Italy.

On his way to England, Melia stopped in Turin and had a providential encounter. There he met a young priest who had lately finished his studies in the University of Turin and was looking around for some missionary enterprise. Melia told him about Pallotti and his ideals and Dr. Faa di Bruno—for it was he—decided to go down to Rome and see for himself.

Melia's intention in going to London was not to dedicate himself exclusively to the spiritual care of the Italian colony there. He wanted, like St. Paul of the Cross and the Venerable Dominic Barbieri before him, to convert the British people back to Catholicism, but he first must see to it that the faith of his fellow-countrymen was saved. He became the chaplain of the Italian colony and organized schools, missions and retreats for them; he defended them before the magistrates and in the public press. A year after his arrival in London he was joined by Faa di Bruno who had gone to Rome, met Pallotti, thrown in his lot with the Society of the Catholic Apostolate and then, wanting to be a missionary, left with Pallotti's consent for England.

The two men found that there was a great deal to be done for Catholicism, not only in saving the faith of the Italians, but in preaching and teaching the faith to non-Catholics. These were stirring times in the religious life of England: the Oxford Movement was quivering in the air and the Catholics who had survived the Reformation were emerging from their ghetto-like isolation. Melia and Faa di Bruno wrote their impressions to Pallotti, whose interest and delight in this outpost of the Society of the Catholic Apostolate is reflected in the long and revealing correspondence he maintained with them till his death. He is interested in everything: the Oxford converts for whom he offers to secure such spiritual favors in Rome as they may desire; the apostolic outlook of the English Catholic clergy; the plans for a church for the London Italians; the spiritual life of his subjects; the progress of the movement for the reestablishment of the hierarchy—in which event Melia, an old Propaganda hand, played a part whose details are not sufficiently known even yet. In the light of all the information transmitted to him, Pallotti undertakes to draw the attention of the rectors of the colleges in Rome to the new conditions which are manifesting themselves in England so that they may modify the training of the students accordingly; he rejoices when he learns that there are two English priests who are desirous of joining the Society.

Dr. Faa di Bruno was first appointed to be the spiritual director of a community of recent converts, who had joined the Church with their leader, Frederick Faber. These were the Wilfridians, who shortly afterwards merged with the Oratorians introduced by Newman into England. Faa di Bruno then took up the life of a pioneer missionary, first at Kentish Town, then at Barnet and later at Highgate, and in his spare moments, which were not many, he helped Melia with the Italian colony which was centered around Holborn. They had no house and no church and the necessities of this flock were such that these buildings had to be erected in one of the most expensive neighborhoods of London, and the funds had to come from one of the poorest communities in that city.

Vincent helped. There was still some money left from his family patrimony so he sent his subjects fifteen hundred pounds. The future church, he laid it down, was to be conducted after the fashion of churches in Rome, with special attention to liturgical detail, the services were to be open to all comers, the church was to be the property of the Society for the purposes of its apostolate and the good of the Italian residents.

On three occasions he was invited to go to London. The first invitation came from Bishop (later Cardinal) Wiseman who wanted at one time to put Pallotti in charge of a special seminary he was thinking of setting up for the training of convert clergymen for the priesthood. It appeared to Wiseman that these converts would receive much benefit from contact with a Roman priest of tact, judgment and sanctity, and who better than Pallotti? The latter consulted his spiritual director, as was his invariable rule before making any important decision of this sort, and the advice received was that there were important commitments in Rome which Pallotti must conduct personally. A second invitation from Wiseman was postponed for later decision and then came Pallotti's death. The third invitation was made during the Roman Revolution by an English spiritual son of Pallotti, named Stephen Tempest, who will recur again in our story.

Father Florence Hardinge Ivers, an English priest who had lived in Rome and became acquainted with Pallotti there, had opened a chapel at his private home in Kentish Town and wished to hand it over to the Society, to serve as a center for mission preaching and other apostolic enterprises. The offer never materialized, but it gave rise to the publication of a note in *The Tablet*, whose praise of his person would have pained Vincent if he had ever got to know of it. It said:

"One of the most remarkable symptoms of the present age is the increase of congregations and pious unions of secular priests, who, though bound by no vow, live together after the fashion of the apostles and the primitive church, devoting their lives to the labors of the apostolic ministry. Among the societies of this nature, founded of late years with the formal sanction of the Holy See, is that formed by Don Vincenzo Pallotti, a venerable priest living in Rome in the odor of sanctity.... Don Vincenzo Pallotti has given directions to Dr. Faa, who belongs to this Society, to join Mr. Ivers at Kentish Town; and thus these ecclesiastics, whose number will be increased as soon as circumstances may permit it, will form the nucleus, it is hoped, of what will prove in the course of years a flourishing branch of the Society. The Society of secular priests, founded by Don Vincenzo Pallotti, is under the special patronage of Our Lady Queen of Apostles...."

The number of permanent recruits for the work of the Society was growing and Vincent determined that it was necessary to draft a rule which would define their state of life and the type of community engagement which was expected of each member. This was completed in manuscript in the year 1846 and is a very full document. Before putting it into execution, he sought the opinions of several wise and holy persons, as was his practice, and it was then submitted to a process of modifications, which was still in progress at the time of his death. It may be that he was unwilling to impose the rule definitively until the community became larger in number and greater collective experiences of its details would then be available.

Simple affection for the founders of their organizations has sometimes led their biographers into making exaggerated claims regarding the originality of the rules which these have drafted. No one can really invent anything new in the Church of God. But it is also true that the great doctrinal and ascetical practices of Catholicism, which have been in it *ab ovo* from the beginning, can be and at various moments of history have been, the objects of special emphasis and the impulse giving rise to this emphasis has arisen from the revelations and inspirations which God gives to His saints. There is no need to claim originality for any of the provisions which Vincent laid down in his Rule but we can very legitimately inquire into the special emphasis which is contained in its substance, and into the relevance which this emphasis bears to the time in which he lived, and to our own times.

In the first place, Vincent views the whole life of the Christian on this earth as a theater of war, in which the forces of good and evil are engaged in perpetual struggle. The individual man, and the religious societies which men create, will only succeed in winning this struggle by *adhering* to our Lord, that is, by the concrete imitation of Jesus Christ in all the situations in which men find themselves implicated. The man who has penetrated the significance of the Gospels and adheres without any reservation to what they teach, is the man who, faced here and now by this or that alternative, can make his concrete choice in the light of that knowledge and that adhesion. The life of the Society of the Catholic Apostolate is to be a life of imitation of Christ.

Next, Vincent lays down that his followers must possess a disposition of mind which he calls "the spirit of sacrifice"; by which term he means a constant engagement in the repression of the ignoble impulses which lurk in the hearts of all men. The contemporary reader may be put off by this word repression which so much psychoanalysis and psychiatry have made very unpopular to the modern ear, but it should be taken in a much larger pattern, for it was one of Pallotti's very earlier principles of spiritual conduct, as we have seen at the beginning of this work, that vices are repressed and finally cast out, by the cultivation of virtue. Nobody in his sound senses will dispute this principle, though there may not be agreement as to how to work it out in practice, or even as to what really constitutes a vice or a virtue.

Vincent then incorporated in his rule what he calls the principle of "spiritual infancy." This does not mean, as at first sight it might appear to do, that his followers are to attempt to live as though they were mentally little children; such would be ridiculous and, furthermore, impossible for adult people. His idea is that the great virtues of the Christian life, such as obedience, affection, kindness, simplicity and so on should be seized on, held and cultivated and increased by way of the same uncomplicated and direct approach with which the child accepts the teachings and the influences of his parents and of the society in which he is placed. It is a great principle, very necessary in this time in which the Christian must live lovingly in a world smouldering with hate, truthfully in a world riddled by propaganda, chastely in a world supercharged with incitations to lust.

He next lays down the principle of "the spirit of the Holy Family of Nazareth." A religious organization, like all organizations made and composed of men, must have its jurisdiction, its authority and its subordinations, for it is in the nature of man to make rules for his societies. But the approaches of subordinates and superiors to rules may be very different, as one can see at first glance by reflecting on such institutions as armies and prisons, and contrasting them with such higher forms of organized society as hospitals and schools. The "approach" which Vincent Pallotti wished his followers to have in regard to their community living their subordinations and their superiorities is nothing less than the "approach" which his meditations discovered in that unique and singular first social and Christian cell: the Holy Family of Nazareth.

He also wished that his Society should be an active apostolic organization, that is, an organization not only created to bear witness, to be "present" in human society, but made also for the purpose of gravitating by positive effort and by positive means on the surrounding world. "The Society," he kept on saying, "must dedicate itself to the multiplication of spiritual and temporal means for the purpose of reviving faith and spreading charity throughout the world." Apostolic activity was to be its criterion of selection. Faced with alternative courses of conduct, the follower of Vincent Pallotti must ask himself: which of these courses is more likely to tend to the multiplication of spiritual and temporal means of apostolic activity, and having made his judgment, he must select the more positive course.

He desired as well that his Society should have a Marian character, and for that reason he placed it under the protection of Our Lady Queen of Apostles. Not that he intended his organization to be dedicated exclusively to the dissemination of the great Marian dogmas among the people, dogmas which inevitably and with the strictest logic lead God's people, by easy and loving pathways, to the Redeemer and to the Trinity. It was rather that he wished his followers to carry out their apostolic work under precisely that type of leadership which Christian piety in all the ages has discerned in that great scene when the Holy Spirit descended on the apostles, who were present in the Upper Room "with Mary, his mother."

And finally, he wished that this Society should be a priestly one. In a very clear fashion Vincent realized that the ills of the Church in his days were not in the last resort traceable to the attacks of her enemies, although these were grave and ominous. The Church has never been afraid of her enemies; what she has always dreaded is the dissensions, the disunities, the sins and the ignorances of her own children. A laity separated from its clergy, a clergy out of spiritual touch with its hierarchy, a clergy at variance within itself, traversed with misunderstanding between regulars and seculars; these, and particularly the latter, were the evils which faced the Church in his day. Now the priest, in the final analysis, is the man whose function is representative: he is to "stand" between God and man, he is to be "present" at all the significant events in the Christian life — the baptisms, the weddings, the deaths of the believers; he is to "share" in all the good community activities of society, by bringing the message of the Gospel to them all: to the trades unions, to the political organizations, to the armies, to the social and welfare organizations; to everyone and to every place where his voice can reach. That is what we consider he meant by wishing his Society to be a sacerdotal one, bringing all priests closer to one another, "outstripping each other in charity" as he used to say with great frequency.

Vincent had just settled in with his community in San Salvatore when Gregory XVI passed away and a new Pope was elected. This was Cardinal Mastai-Ferretti, known better to history as Pius IX, who was to reign longer than St. Peter, and longest of any Pope in history. Mastai-Ferretti spent his youth in Rome and Vincent knew him well. It is said that before entering the ranks of the clergy, Mastai-Ferretti was thinking of becoming a Papal Noble Guard, and one day Vincent told him enigmatically, "You will not guard, but you will be guarded." And here now was the solution of the enigma!

During the few years of life which were left to Vincent, Pius IX showed several signal examples of the favor with which he regarded Pallotti and his community. The first of those was at the solemn closure of the Epiphany Octave of 1847.

"This year (says a contemporary English newspaper published in Rome) the Octave of the Epiphany has enjoyed its most splendid and memorable moment, when the Pontiff in person, wishing to reward the zeal of Pallotti and the devotion of the members of the Catholic Apostolate on account of the marvelous results it has achieved for the missions, the propagation of the faith and the good of the people, presented himself at the church for the closing ceremonies of the Octave."

The visit was unexpected and the immense congregation, more than ten thousand people, was thrilled to see the Pope enter the great church and walk straight to the preaching platform, which he ascended and delivered the sermon in person. It was at that time quite exceptional for the Pope to preach, except for the homilies which were delivered on stated occasions, so he was listened to with hushed attention. He spoke in glowing terms of Pallotti and his work and then went on to exhort his hearers to live to the full the lessons they were learning during the course of the Octave. (A full summary of his discourse on this occasion was prepared and published in the newspaper mentioned just now. The English version was made by Dr. Tobias Kirby and it is the best text we possess of the discourse.)

When the service finished the Pope went into the sacristy, where he received the attendant clergy and among them, Pallotti. His Holiness was elated by the extraordinary attendance of people and congratulated Pallotti on the visible success of his efforts. When he was told that over six thousand people had received Communion during the course of the Octave—a considerable number indeed in the age when Communion was not as frequent as it is now—he asked Vincent if he was satisfied, and observing from his manner that he was not, he remarked cheerfully to the attendant ecclesiastics: "There you are: I knew that Don Vincenzo would not be satisfied anyhow."

Vincent was not satisfied; he had in fact his grave doubts and his reserves about the course which events were likely to take in the city. He knew Rome very well and its people — was not he one of them and did not he spend his days going around among them? He knew the dark and secret forces which were gathering strength to deal a decisive blow, as they hoped, at the Papacy and at the Catholic religion.

Pius IX had come to the papal throne with the reputation of a liberal-minded man who was not in sympathy with the austere, repressive policy of his predecessors. The other Italian principalities at this period, sensing the approach of revolution, were taking measures, more or less timid, more or less overt, in order to stem the tide before it became overwhelming. The measures tended towards giving the people a larger participation in the affairs of government, a greater control over the spending of money and the making of the laws; good policies in themselves so long as the new power did not pass into the hands of conspirators and plotters who were not concerned about the people but wanted simply to wrest the power from the princes and take it themselves, for which purpose they sought to conceal it at all costs.

Pius IX had to be convinced by hard experience that the demagogues who approached him with fair words and fairer promises were not the unselfish patriots that they pretended to be. Time had to pass before it became clear that these demagogues were really being managed by obscure evil forces so far in the background that many people did not even believe that they existed at all. But Pallotti was not for one moment deceived because he had early seen the havoc which was being wrought in many souls by the subtle poison. But it is too early to deal with this part of our story. Let us continue with our account of the munificences of Pius IX towards the Society of the Catholic Apostolate.

On two of these we must dwell a moment. Vincent's society of priests of the Catholic Apostolate was still a tiny organization, founded thus far on the principle of voluntary association. Strictly speaking it did not have, under the canon law, any rights and any privileges. In order to secure its juridical status Vincent approached Pope Pius IX with a very ample petition indeed; that the Society of priests of the Catholic Apostolate should be granted all the privileges which the Church had at various times granted to the Regular Orders and Congregations! It was a very considerable request, for the privileges were many, and had been acquired over the centuries by the most venerable bodies in the Church, and here now was this newly-born Society, whose exact juridical nature was not as yet defined by any document from the Church, demanding an equal share in those ancient privileges. In his petition, Vincent adduced two reasons for his request; one, that it was necessary to promote "regular observance," that is, an orderly and uniform method of procedure, in the houses of the community; and secondly, that the concession would be advantageous for the works of the apostolic ministry and the salvation of souls. On September 2, 1847, Pius IX granted under his own signature the request which had been made to him. We may rest assured in concluding that the Holy Father relied on what he knew about Vincent Pallotti, his aims and his methods, when he took his pen and signed his assent to the very unusual request. And the unfolding of events, which has finally led to the canonization of Vincent Pallotti, has given its justification to the imaginative vision of Vincent and the trusting generosity of the Pope.

The papal concession referred to the Society's share in the spiritual privileges and the various indulgences and participation of merits which the Church had bestowed on various orders by virtue of the splendid doctrines of the communion of saints and the Mystical Body of the Lord on earth. Surely it referred as well to the concrete privileges of jurisdiction and of legal competence which the Popes had granted in the course of time to the other communities; but legalists might not be entirely satisfied. Someone may have voiced a doubt, raised a question, as to the correct interpretation of the papal concession, for Vincent found it necessary to recur a second time to the Holy Father, praying for a clarification. This was made by the Holy Father in March of 1849, during his stay at Gaeta. The document makes it clear that the concession of privileges accorded in the first instance referred not only to purely spiritual favors, but also to juridical privileges, including the very notable one known as exemption.

At the beginning of this work we have quoted some opinions whose burden was that Vincent was considered by some people as a "bad influence" on the Pope. They were thinking and speaking from a political angle, in which Pallotti had no interest at all. His concern was with souls and with the sharp decline in religious practice. Nevertheless, acting under advice, he gave up the frequent audiences which in the beginning he had had with the Holy Father. "Under the present circumstances," he wrote on August 28, 1848, to a friend, "prudence requires that I should not visit the Holy Father; I have not been in audience since April 6."

Pius IX decided to grant a Constitution to the Papal States, which provided for a democratic representation of the people in the government and at the same time guaranteed the rights of the papacy. It was so fair and equable a settlement that if it had been accepted with goodwill it would undoubtedly have worked, but that was not what the sectarians wanted. Their plans included public agitation, repression by the government, revolution and finally the overthrow of the papacy and of religion. The news that the new Pope was a "liberal" brought a flock of people into Rome and its neighborhood, intent on carrying out their plans as soon as possible. Now the city of Rome was a well-policed place and it was not so easy to stir up trouble under the noses of the guardians of the law; there was better hunting to be had in the towns and villages which surrounded the city. It was largely on these places that the city depended for its supplies, and trouble in them could easily be converted into trouble in Rome. For this reason the sectarians devoted much effort to spreading their ideas and theories among the villagers. Pallotti knew the temper and the dispositions of these village dwellers very well, for his church was a great resort for them during their visits to Rome. We find it very significant that from 1846 onwards the Society of the Catholic Apostolate, in spite of its exiguous numbers, gave a large number of missions and retreats in these villages and towns. Vincent himself took part in as many of them as he could fit into his schedule of work. The point at issue was in no wise a political one; it was a question of saving the faith of these people who were being led astray by experienced agitators.

The Parliament of the Papal States went into session in the month of November, 1848, and at the very first meeting the Prime Minister whom the Pope had appointed, Count de Rossi, was assassinated on his way to the Chambers; the revolutionary sector made its attitude quite plain by refusing to suspend the session, though the Prime Minister had been attacked on the very stairs leading to the building. It was soon clear to everybody that the papal policy had failed.

CHAPTER VI

The Closing Scenes

The revolutionaries prepared their ground by involving in their toils respected members of the clergy. They hoped to neutralize in that way the influence of religion among the people.

There was a famous Piedmontese priest, Vincenzo Gioberti, who was deep in their councils and came to Rome in order to assist the cause as far as he understood it. "For his own political ends," writes Melia, "Gioberti invited Pallotti to visit him." Vincent's reply was that he had not time to pay visits because he was too busy with his priestly duties. Gioberti then sent to say that he would himself call upon Pallotti, at whatever time suited him. The reply was that he still was too busy.

The revolutionary leaders finally compelled the sovereign Pontiff to put his signature to their appointments as Ministers of the Papal States. He soon found himself in an untenable position. He withdrew to the Quirinal and took no further part in public affairs. The revolutionaries put a guard on the palace to prevent his escape.

On the afternoon of November 24th of the year 1848 the Ambassador of France called on the Pope. The guards posted by the revolutionaries wondered at the great length of the audience; they did not know that the Pontiff had retired to his private apartments while the Ambassador sat quietly in the papal study. The Pope then laid aside his papal robes and dressed in the ordinary garb of a priest, made his

146

way out of the palace by an unfrequented doorway, where a hackney cab waited for him and his servant. He was driven by devious routes to a deserted quarter near the Colosseum, where the carriage of the Bavarian Ambassador waited. Here the Pontiff changed carriages, drove to the city gates, the Ambassador's passport enabling them to get past the guards, and the carriage set out for Naples. For the third time in living memory, a Pope had been forced to leave Rome.

The revolutionaries were at first chagrined and than became elated, when they observed that the reactions of the population showed no signs of menace to themselves. The priests of the Catholic Apostolate were then forbidden to preach in the Military Hospital and to hold services for the soldiers; confessions and communions were discouraged among them. Little by little the pressure was increased and in the end the priests were thrown out altogether.

The Roman Republic was eventually proclaimed and though the revolutionaries professed the greatest respect for religion as such, the pattern we know so well of persecution of the clergy was employed, until a point was reached when it became dangerous for a priest to appear in his robes in public. Very dangerous indeed, for about thirty of them were murdered in the streets.

One day Vincent had occasion to cross the great square in front of the Quirinal Palace, from which the Pope had fled; the place was guarded and one of the soldiers lifted his musket and fired point-blank at the priest, but, unaccountably, Vincent was not hit. It seemed best for the community in San Salvatore to disperse, and so they did after a three-day retreat. Vincent found refuge in the Irish College of Rome, which, being a foreign institution, offered a prospect (mistaken as it proved) of security.

Here he stayed for five months, employing his time in prayer, in giving advice to those who learned where he was and sought him out, and in correspondence. Forty years later Archbishop Kirby recalled an incident about Vincent's stay in the Irish College during this period.

"While he stayed at the College it was his habit to invite others into his room to pray with him. I remember that on one occasion, just after breakfast the Abbate S. was thus invited and they prayed together till dinnertime. During the recreation after this meal, the Abbate addressed Pallotti: 'Listen, don't ask me to come and pray with you any more, because I will not be able to come.'"

During Pallotti's stay, the revolutionaries invaded the Irish College, searching for people who might have taken refuge there. They suspected that a certain cardinal was concealed in it, but they would anyhow have been quite pleased to capture Pallotti. They searched the entire College, entered every room, but unaccountably passed over the one where Vincent was lodged, so they did not discover his presence! His followers have always believed that both on this occasion and the other, when the soldier fired on him, God intervened to protect Vincent from violent death at the hands of his misled countrymen.

Kirby also remembered that it was Vincent's gentle practice, on being told of the faults and crimes of anyone, to change the conversation by remarking: "Poverello, let us have pity on him." The expression was often on his lips during the period of the revolution. One day news of a particular atrocious outrage reached the College, and Pallotti inquired if it was known who its authors were. The rector of the College, Msgr. (later Cardinal) Cullen, made the tart remark, "Some of our poverelli, of course!"

There was an Englishman resident in Rome, named Walter Tempest, a member of the ancient Catholic family of Tempest from Broughton Hall in Yorkshire. He had known Pallotti since 1842 and now, for love of him, Tempest asked and received permission to come and stay at the College in order to keep him company. Mr. Tempest wanted to take him to England, offering to pay all the expenses of the journey but Vincent would not go without the advice of his spiritual director who was not available at the moment because he too, one supposes, was in hiding. Mr. Tempest was insistent in his offer, as Pallotti informs Melia in one of his letters to London. In fact, this insistence provoked the only instance known to us of a pun on Pallotti's lips. "The charitable Tempest," he wrote, "*storms me with his kind offer!*"

During the long hours of his seclusion and solitude, Vincent made use of his time in writing letters to various people in which he endeavored to uncover the hidden and mystical meaning of the calamity which was threatening to overwhelm the Church and the Papal States, and exhorting his correspondents to ever greater fidelity to our Lord and greater resignation to His will. One letter was addressed to the chief pastors of the Catholic Church, another to Ferdinand, King of Naples, who was now the custodian of the person of the Holy Father; another to his brethren of the Catholic Apostolate in England, another to priests working on the English mission, and another to the seminarists of the Propaganda College. He also wrote to the nuns of two religious communities who had been roughly thrust out of their monasteries by the revolutionaries who required the buildings for their own purposes. To one of these, the Dominican Nuns of Sts. Dominic and Sixtus, he wrote:

"Create now in your souls a new and richer spiritual monastery. This monastery will consist in possessing God more closely than before.... You can now say: my monastery is God, all God and all His divine attributes and His infinite perfections. The Father, Son and Holy Spirit are your divine monastery. God's infinite power, His wisdom, goodness, mercy and purity, all His infinite perfections are now your monastery from henceforward."

To the Poor Clare Nuns of San Silvestro in Capite he wrote recommending them to bear their sufferings, which he believed to be the greatest so far in their lives, by seeking for the strictest conformity with the will of God; he recalled to them the mystic doctrine that all souls are offered the opportunity to imitate in some way in their own lives the sufferings of Christ on this earth. "The more we are mortified and suffer lovingly to imitate Him in His suffering, the more grace we will be granted to perform the works of eternal life."

The Catholic rulers of Europe decided at last to restore order in the Papal States. French troops disembarked at Civitavecchia and marched on Rome, arriving at the outskirts of the city on July 1. Writing to Melia, Vincent describes their entry in these terms:

"Defenses, barricades, arms, harangues to make the people rise, lies and other deceitful tricks were all used to prevent the entry of the French. On the night of Sunday, July 1, a French General marched in with three hundred men.... Many people, even good people, including women, some of whom were seen going about armed with rifles, were alarmed at the coming of the French, for they had been told that everybody would be killed and their goods stolen, except the priests and nuns.... Near the bridge of Quattro Capi the General went ahead with sixty men and ran into five or six hundred revolutionaries. The General thought he and his troops would be slaughtered, but the revolutionaries opened their ranks and let them pass.... That same day the formal entry of the remaining troops took place."

Some time had to elapse before the population could return to its normal ways. The letter from which we quote, which was written a week after the entry of the French, goes on to say:

"Some have shown their evil dispositions by sneaking up and stabbing priests, French soldiers and people, not many, in all about twenty. Everything had been prepared so that at their arrival the French would find the streets littered with dead, and it is a miracle this did not happen."

The community of the Catholic Apostolate was broken up during the emergency period. Some took refuge in Naples, others in the country. The report went about that there were great treasures stored in the house attached to the church, but a searcher soon found out his mistake.

The troubled city slowly settled down and calm returned, but Pallotti was not satisfied with the indecision and irresolution which was showing itself among the members of the provisional government.

"I venture to write to you (he says to Cardinal Lambruschini) regarding the need of a decided, universal, complete and stable policy. I fear that (as appears from some maneuvers already made in Rome) we shall end up with half measures, which always terminate badly."

This extract shows that Vincent had a plan, whose application would solve the problems of his times. We hasten to say that this plan, which is outlined in his letter to the chief pastors of the Church, has little or nothing to do with the temporalities of this world, for his mind was not engaged with the problems of finance and economy, or the best methods of governing mankind.

Vincent's world was a supernatural world and the evils of the age were to his mind due to man's contempt and neglect of the values which that kind of world carries with it. The attitudes of men must be changed, and first of all the attitudes of those who were most responsible for the preservation and the increase of these values; that is, the pastors of the Church. Consider the enumeration he makes of the chief evils of his day, in that letter which he wrote to the chief pastors of the Church from his room in the Irish College.

In the first place, he makes the reflection that at this time the supernatural world is threatened not by one particular heresy, but by a whole constellation of them. To the average Italian Catholic person in that age, the word "heresy" would probably bring up before the mind some image of Protestantism or of one of the ancient rejected doctrines such as Nestorianism or Arianism. But at the very time that Pallotti was writing, the most destructive heresies the world has yet seen were incubating in Northern Europe; in one corner of which sat Karl Marx cogitating how to destroy the doctrine of God's existence by disseminating the persuasion that this very doctrine is the main obstacle to mankind's happiness and progress; in another place in the same continent a man of scientific bent was pondering how to exclude Him from the record of man's slow ascent and to replace Him with such terms as natural selection and the survival of the fittest. But the weapon of truth was in the hands of the Church and it was urgently necessary to employ it at that moment in an unusual and extraordinary way.

The second great evil of his times which Pallotti felt must be checked at all costs, is one to which modern sensibility has become deadened: the evil of blasphemy. How far we have gone along this road of complacency may be gauged by the simple fact that in our time the rulers of great nations have dedicated themselves and their peoples officially and publicly to the proposition that there is no God and have employed their immense resources and power in spreading this tenet all over the world, while the believing nations whose rulers from time to time proclaim their faith in God take this immense negation in their stride and go ahead as though nothing had been said or done against the majesty of God. A startled reaction here and there in some church group, a learned work or two, some newspaper articles and that is all. No man who has experienced God and His sanctity and His love can do otherwise than regard the denial of His existence or the derision of His majesty as the most terrible of all sins. So it was with Pallotti, who a year after his ordination to the priesthood made a vow that he would kiss the floor in the solitude of his room in reparation for any blasphemy he should chance to hear. To bring home to Catholics the gravity of this awful vice and the necessity of making public reparation for it, he established at different times various sodalities and confraternities directed to that purpose and to the glorification of God's holy name.

The next great evil which Vincent discerns in his day was the decline of truthfulness among the rulers of the world. "Instead of the law, impiety and lies have come out of Sion." How right he was! The time, however, was yet to come when the very name of the great institution with which he was connected for so many years of his life—the Propaganda—was to be taken over and used as the label for all the official lies which, in war and in peace, destroy charity and peace among men and poison with the virus of hatred all social relations among the peoples.

Another great evil which he denounced with apostolic freedom was the neglect into which the pastoral office had fallen; bishops and superiors, through timidity, carelessness or ignorance, were failing to use the means and methods which are placed in their hands for looking after their flocks, such as the holding of Synods and the making of visitations of their charges.

And then he goes on to state what he believes will be the only efficacious and permanent remedy:

"In the reigns of the Pontiffs of holy memory, Pius VI, Pius VII and in the beginning of the Pontificate of Gregory XVI, the Lord spoke to us in His anger and His mercy (he is alluding to the imprisonments and the revolts against the authority of these Popes) but things went from bad to worse. Now once more the Lord has spoken in His wrath and His mercy. The time is therefore at hand for more efficacious and more universal remedies to be applied, so that all the orders of persons in the Church of God, namely, the clergy, the religious orders and God's people be brought to a sense of their duty. The way to do this is to convoke a general council of the Church."

This is not the first time in Pallottian literature that a general council of the Church appears in his thought as the solution for the grave and pressing problems of the Church. In the letter, written in the year 1840, to be read after his death by his collaborators, after speaking of the urgent necessities of the Church and the possible solutions, he adds:

"A general council of the Church, called and presided by a Pope, would certainly be of enormous utility to the Church, but how many difficulties in the way! A beginning could be made...by a more faithful observance, by both clergy and people, of the existing laws and the dispositions of the Council of Trent."

The Pallottian concept is, then, that in the order of the world the acceptance and observance of the supernatural values and ordinances are the key happiness and salvation. If these values and ordinances are properly taught and properly observed, men will be happy. If men honor and love God, they will honor and love one another. If men reverence the Blessed Virgin, then they will reverence all women. The perfect man is Jesus Christ and the closer men imitate Him, the more perfect they will become. That is the beginning and the end of man's unceasing search for perfection.

It might be thought that a man whose whole mind was taken up and his thinking shaped in the rarified climate of these high and mystic ideas must have lived out of this world; in the stratosphere, beyond the clouds. But it was not so. For while one sector of his thought ranged through these incommensurable regions, another sector was keenly occupied with the practical details of living; how to send one thousand Roman crowns to Melia in London without losing too much in the exchange; how the house attached to the Italian Church in London should be built with sufficient amplitude so that the Fathers might be able to offer hospitality to other priests; whether it would be suitable to send a couple of masons from Rome in order to help with the building in London; how a power-of-attorney to be executed in Rome had better be drafted in the English language in London so as to avoid unnecessary expense; how he himself will look after the stringing of a gift of rosaries for the poor provided that he gets the beads, and so on — his correspondence is full of practical good sense and down-to-earth detail.

His hopes for reform through the agency of a general council were finally realized after his death. But twenty irrecoverable years had passed; the problems had grown so much greater by 1869, when the First Vatican Council was summoned by Pius IX. The great task was commenced but the fall of the tottering temporal power was imminent and the Council was adjourned before any of the practical details could be taken up: the details which would have helped enormously to infuse new life into the whole organism.

When the situation was restored after the entry of the French troops, Vincent had not much time left. He took up all the threads of his usual activities, the Society returned to its work in the military hospital, to the preaching of missions, the care of the House of Charity. The number of aspirants to join the community was growing and there was not much room left in the house next to the church. Vincent set about hunting for another house which could serve as a novitiate in the outskirts of Rome; there were two places which appeared suitable and he tried to obtain first one and then the other, fruitlessly. He was also taken up with the new foundation of the House of Charity in the town of Velletri. He was a man very respectful of law and the rights of others and he was exceedingly careful all his life to fulfill scrupulously even the smallest legal formalities. None of the transactions in which he was concerned was ever successfully questioned and he took pains to have all the necessary documents preserved. He was a prudent and wise manager who was scrupulous about doing everything properly. On at least one occasion his successors had signal reason to bless him for his foresight, when, fifteen years after his death someone wished to deprive the Society of an important piece of property in London, and on examination of the documents it was found that Pallotti had secured the rights of the community against precisely that very contingency, in a manner which ordinary prudence would have considered at the time as excessively scrupulous. But time was running out, and he knew it. While he was hidden in the Irish College during the dark days of May 1849 he made a note in his diary recording that he was fifty-five years old. Never before had he made any reference to length of life in this book.

"My God...through an incomprehensible prodigy of Your infinite mercy You have allowed me to live till the present moment. For fifty-five years Your infinite mercies have been granted to me.... My God, what shall I do with the remainder of my life? I knownot how to speak...."

And he goes on to quote the words of Scripture: "Come my beloved, come, hasten, come and do not delay."

At the end of November of the year 1849 he made his last retreat, for which, as was his habit, he withdrew to the retreat-house of the Vincentian Fathers in Rome, in a building which is now part of the Italian parliament.

"My God (he writes in his Diary), my infinite mercy, I come to Your house full of confusion. I do not know what I ought to do. I do not know how to make these holy exercises, I do not know what profit to extract from them."

He once more reminds himself that he is fifty-five years old, and as if closing an account which was opened long ago, when he declared that God and God alone was to be his objective, not intellect, nor will, nor food, nor drink, nor air, nor anything of this world, he proceeds to ask himself whether he has used any of these things as ends in themselves whereas they should merely have been instruments.

"Tell us, Vincent, how have you profited from the infinite love of God? ...How have you profited from the gift of free will? ...How have you abused the powers of the soul and the feelings of the body.... What use have you made of health? ...How have you profited from sickness? ...Have you used the light of this world in order to contemplate and love the inextinguishable light of God?... Have you profited of food and drink in order to hunger and thirst after God, who is the true food and drink of our souls?... Have you used all the objects of God's creation as God has wished you to do?... How often have you made use of the things created by God in order to damage your own soul and give scandal to your neighbor?"

Who can hope to penetrate fully the secret of any human being who is very near to God? At this point Vincent's Diary reveals a stage in his life when the overwhelming attraction of the Divinity overpowers his soul; in the next motion of his spirit he pleads his own unworthiness and then goes on to glorify God because His own infinite goodness compels God Himself to overcome this obstacle of human unworthiness. Here is a passage of singular beauty taken from his Diary at this time:

"My God, You let me live and You communicate all that You are, Unity and Trinity, in order to transform me into Yourself, to become one thing with the Father, Son and Holy Spirit. My God, because of what I am and because of what You are, I am bound to say: depart from me, O Lord, for I am a sinful man; and at the same time I must ask You: Come Lord, do not delay, because I cannot stay a moment without You. And at the same time, O Lord, in order to express myself I cannot avoid saying that I suffer with You, because the infinite love with which from all eternity You have loved me freely and mercifully, obliges You to come to me, to stay with me, and to make me one with You. My God, Your love leads You into excesses.... Come, O my beloved, come, hasten, come and do not delay. One thing consoles me for this excess of love, ever ancient and ever new, in every moment of my life, for all eternity Your infinite love will be glorified...."

In this final period of his life he wrote a paraphrase on the great canticle of the Benedicite. It commences with the thought which so often occurs in his meditations: the destruction of self to be replaced by our Lord.

"Jesus my Lord (he writes), cast me out and place here Yourself; may my life and every work of mine be destroyed, and let Your life be my life."

Then he goes on, he who so often dwelt upon the Gospel texts of the holy Infancy and the public life of our Lord, to seek a new term of assimilation with the Redeemer:

"Let Your agony be my agony, Your death my death, Your resurrection my resurrection, Your ascension my ascension. May all that is You be also mine. May the life of the Blessed Trinity be my life."

The impression is conveyed that he is now seeking the final assimilation of his own life to the life of Christ: that in his mind the thought of his own imminent death is now accepted and used as an active element in his desire for the total union with God.

There is an unusual feature about this Benedicite which attracts our attention. The idea of his death is introduced in the very first verse; the second verse speaks of his birth and the text continues with his Baptism, and the other facts of his life. The normal place to refer to his death would have been at the end of the canticle. But Pallotti here places it at the beginning!

All the external evidence which was collected by his followers points to some foreknowledge of his death, at least after his farewell to the Venerable Bernardo Clausi. The latter, about whom we shall have occasion to speak again, paid a visit to Vincent before leaving for Calabria where he proposed to spend some time. The old friends exchanged little gifts: Vincent gave Clausi a snuff-box; Clausi gave Vincent a packet of snuff. Part of a little dialogue between them has been preserved, couched in the elliptic speech of those who know each other very well; they conversed using ordinary expressions whose undertones conveyed a message deeper than the words themselves.

"Vincent, I am going. What about you? What are you doing on this wretched earth?"

"So you are going, Bernardo. Where do you want to go?"

"I am going to visit grandfather and grand-mother." (Bernardo Clausi was going to Paola, where the parents of St. Francis of Paola, founder of his Order, were buried). There was a silence, and then Clausi said:

"Remember, Vincent, we shall meet above, after a month and three days." Vincent's death took place exactly one month and three days after that of Clausi.

Vincent went about his ordinary tasks much as usual, but a few unusual details were noticed by the loving hearts who surrounded him. The celebrations for the Octave of the Epiphany, which had been omitted the year before on account of the Revolution were organized as usual, but this year Vincent did not himself take charge; he appointed another priest to be director of the Octave; the first time he ever did so. He carefully made out a written list of the benefactors whose alms he used to collect every year to help cover the Octave expenses, with their addresses; also a new departure. When the Octave was finished and had proved a great success, some people were congratulating him on the good results; he thanked them, and said: "Next year you will do it yourselves." A day or so later he went to visit an old friend, who was ill and had not been able to attend the Epiphany that year; when they were saying goodbye, Vincent said: "Don't worry about me any more. You understand? Don't worry about me any more."

On January 14, he went to say Mass in the church of the Sacred Heart Sisters, the stately edifice which stands at the top of the famous landmark in Rome known as the Spanish Steps. During the Mass he preached what was to be his last sermon, on the Mother Most Admirable, at whose altar the Mass was celebrated. One of the sisters present took a few notes of the sermon, in which Pallotti drew, she wrote, special attention to the lily which in this picture our Lady holds in her hands. When Vincent was taking his leave, he said to the Mother Superior: "We shall not meet again."

Later that day he called on the community of the Pallottine Sisters at the House of Charity, and on the following day, he said Mass at the Monastery of Divine Love on the Esquiline Hill and then went for lunch to the home of Salvati, the faithful benefactor who had so reluctantly taken up that collection which proved decisive for the foundation of the Society. It was realized afterwards that these were really farewell visits.

During the lunch he felt ill. "God does not wish me to eat. I am feverish," he said. A carriage was summoned and he returned home. That evening a man called, with whom he had made an appointment. Hearing that Vincent was unwell, the man, who wished to make his confession, said that he would return another day, but Vincent insisted on seeing him, remarking, "Tomorrow will be too late."

On January 16, he said his last Mass in the little domestic oratory and returned to bed. The doctor was called and the illness was diagnosed: pleurisy, very dangerous in the case of a patient with weakened lungs. The doctor ordered a great number of medicines and Vincent protested that it was not worthwhile spending so much on medicines in his case. (The medicines were actually provided cost-free, by an old school-friend chemist who besought the privilege as a great favor.)

The Venerable Elizabeth Sanna, to whom we will refer later on, came to inquire how he was, and he instructed the priest who was bearing him company to say, "I shall soon leave my bed." The priest joyfully interpreted the message to mean that he would soon be well enough to leave his bed, but when Elizabeth Sanna heard the exact words of the message, she was afflicted. "Don Vincenzo means that he is going to die, for he cannot take his bed to the grave with him."

All his life Vincent showed an extraordinary devotion to the sacrament of Penance, and now, on his deathbed, his fervor was multiplied, for he asked for it several times a day.

On Sunday, January 20, he received the Viaticum, surrounded by his sorrowing friends and by the priests of the community. One of them asked him to pray for the Society. He uttered the prayer: "A blessing of goodness and of wisdom on the Society…" and his voice failed him. Noticing that the priests still stayed with him, and recollecting that this was Sunday and that there would be many people waiting to go to confession in the church, the apostolic flame which consumed him all his life flared up: "There are people waiting; go down and attend to them."

On the evening of the Sunday he received Extreme Unction and then appeared to improve, so much so that the priests attending him considered that it was no longer necessary for him to make his final dispositions, as he proposed, regarding the affairs of the Society, but he insisted.

For many years Vincent kept in his library a little book containing prayers for a happy death and in 1843 he drew the attention of one of his companions to this book, saying: "I want you to read this to me when I am on my deathbed." He had been seriously ill several times since that date, but he never asked for it. Now he did so, and poor Father Vaccari—he was to succeed Vincent as Superior General of the Society—realized that in spite of appearances the end was at hand. "What will happen to us now?" he asked in his despair. "The Society will fall to pieces without you." Vincent's answer, clear and distinct and sweet as the peal of a silver bell, has heartened all his followers in many trials for over a century. "The Society will live and will be blessed by God." And he went on to say that his death would assist it to live. This Father Vaccari was a man of deep feelings who had loved Vincent tenderly—in order to follow him he had given up the prospects of a great career—and his affection made him importunate. "Father Vincent," he said at one moment during the last day, "God will hear you if you ask Him to let you live a while longer." But Vincent's answer was final: "Let me go where God calls me."

On the afternoon before his death, Elizabeth Sanna again called for news; Vincent was told of the visit and he said: "Tell her that tomorrow is a great feast in heaven"—January 23 was, according to the Roman Calendar, the feast of the Espousals of our Lady—and this illiterate mendicant woman understood the significance of the cryptic message like a flash. "I understand. Tell Don Vincenzo that I understand." And she went back to her solitary little room to mourn him.

He died at a quarter to nine on the evening of January 22, after living fifty-five years, nine months and one day.

For three days the little people and the great, the poor and the rich, the prelates and the priests visited his remains as they lay in state in the little church—many thousands of people, who demanded relics of the dead, who touched their rosaries and their medals to the remains in the open coffin. They mourned him and they began to pray to him immediately, for with the sure Catholic intuition for such things they knew that they had *seen* sanctity in this man, who had lived so long among them, who had walked their streets and said and done holy things about which they could not be deceived. "Pallotti is a saint," they said.

This was the opinion too of the ecclesiastical authorities, who soon opened the formal investigation which the Church law requires. It was also the conviction of his companions who decided to preserve everything exactly in his room as it was when he lived in it, and to collect every object which he had owned and every scrap of writing which he had ever written. They found to their surprise that other people had been doing just this; that tiny little notes in his handwriting, dealing many of them with trivialities, had been preserved in some cases for forty years, because the recipients even then were aware that this was the writing of no ordinary man and that one day they would become important. One hundred years, to the very day, after his death he was beatified.

No one who believes in the supernatural can be surprised that a man who surrounded his life with supernaturality, who discerned it so swiftly and surely in others, whose true friends were walking on the same paths, would not have passed away without some portent. Elizabeth Sanna was mourning in her little room, when suddenly she saw Vincent embracing the Savior on the cross, illuminated by a light which appeared to shine out of the wounds on the Lord's body. The vision lasted, she thought, for about fifteen minutes, and she marked its end by the tolling of the great bell of St. Peter's, which on the evening of the 22nd of January, 1850, rang at nine o'clock. At the same time a certain Carmelite friar was kneeling in the choir of the church of our Lady of Victories after concluding the evening office. Suddenly this priest, whose name was Father Ignatius, rose to his feet and astonished his companions by saying in a loud voice: "At this moment Vincent Pallotti has gone to heaven." He was asked if he had seen a vision, and he explained that he had not, but that a sudden conviction was imparted to him at that moment, and he had to give it utterance. Vincent's body was laid to rest under the floor of the little church, near to one of the side walls, dressed in priestly vestments. The great care which was taken at the ceremony of the burial showed that everybody concerned realized that all the formalities must be observed very carefully. A leaden tube with official seals identifying the name and titles of the deceased was placed beside the body, which was then enclosed in a triple coffin, each one carefully closed and sealed. The spot was marked with an inscription setting forth who rested there.

Vincent left no wealth behind him. "There was not found with him," says his biographer Melia, "either gold or silver or copper, or anything of value, but only a few worn and patched-up clothes for his own use. Great riches were however found in an assortment of instruments of penance, which are preserved as relics." Vincent's family property was all left to the Society of the Catholic Apostolate, subject to certain rights of maintenance for his surviving brothers.

Very creditable witnesses have stated that for as long as a month after Vincent's death the atmosphere in the room where he died was peculiar, for a sweet smell lingered there, in spite of the open window. And why not? For a saint had passed from there to his glory, and the Lord of all Nature and all Grace has been known to honor before now the places where His saints have inhabited.

It is said, with much justification, that the character of a person can be made out from the books on his shelves. At the very least, the study of someone's collection of books will certainly serve in most cases to illustrate complexities of character which might not otherwise be immediately evident; we would, for instance, be led into a definite train of thought if in the library of an analytical chemist we were to find, besides the textbooks and literature of that branch of knowledge an extensive collection of works of detective fiction; or if the library of a surgeon were found to contain a large assortment of illustrated books of travel. We hasten to add that no problem of diversification crops up during the consideration of the books which Vincent Pallotti left behind him. It is rather their homogeneity which draws our attention.

Vincent's library has been preserved intact as from the moment of his death, and consists of almost two hundred items all told. It is probable that some, and perhaps many books of his were in the hands of other people at the time of his passing, for he was in the habit of loaning books which he considered of interest or of importance to others. For years he kept a register of such books on loan; a manuscript copybook in which he noted down the name of the book, the person to whom it was loaned, and the date of issue and its return, but the register ceased some years before his death, and there is no reason to think that he had interrupted his practice of lending books. From time to time a book turns up with his name in it, but it does not follow that he always wrote his name into his own books. Probably some of his books, unidentified as they were at the time of his death, simply remained in the hands of those who were using them and have now joined the limbo which awaits the current literature of any era when there are no special circumstances or means of identification to make them valuable for extrinsic or intrinsic reasons.

The first impression made by the catalogue of Vincent's books is that this collection was made by a person whose interests were exclusively religious.

There are few historical works among them, no books of the general knowledge type, no works of imagination, no novels, nothing bearing on political philosophy or on science. The only exceptions are a work on astronomy and a couple of pamphlets dealing with the political philosophies of the period, which are here, one would suspect, by some chance. The books all bear on religion and by far the greater part of them are of the "devotional" type. They are nearly all in Italian and Latin; a few in French and a couple in Spanish and one in German. Pallotti must have possessed an adequate knowledge of the French language, for his secondary education was received under the domination of the Napoleonic times, when that language was a "must" all over the Empire. But in his library there is no sign of the penetration of the French culture.

Here is an extract chosen at random from the catalogue of his library:

50. Enchiridion on the Mass, from the works of Benedict XIV;
51. Preparation for Death, by Cardinal Bona;
52. The Life of St. Anthony of Padua;
53. Extracts from Blosius on the Passion of our Lord;
54. Scupoli's Lily of Purity;
55. Suso's Meditations on the Agony of our Lord;
56. Devotion to the Blessed Sacrament, by Lanzi;
57. Novena in honor of St. Rita of Cascia;
58. Chronology of the Popes;
59. The Imitation, by Kempis;
60. The practice of the Presence of God;
61. Purgatory open to the piety of the faithful;
62. The Chinese missionaries of the Jesuit Order;
63. The Spiritual Works of Fr. Pinamonti SJ;
64. Meditations of da Ponte;
65. The month of Mary, for persons living in the world.

It is the library of a person whose interest — we shall not say whose main, but whose *only* interest is in religion. Nor may it be said that it is a religious library got together with any specialized purpose, say for the study of Sacred Scripture, or theology, or any particular branch of religious knowledge; with this exception, however, the user of this library found it necessary to have on hand a good many works on ascetical and mystical theology, as well as manuals for the direction of souls aspiring to the higher life. There are, to be sure, works on Scripture, but they are not of the primarily scientific kind; there are books on ecclesiastical law, but of the kind useful for practical affairs.

On the desk in his bedroom at which he used to pray lay the books which he used most frequently: the "bedside books" as it were:

1. The Mystical City of God, or Life of the Blessed Virgin;
2. Life of the Servant of God Ferdinand Trevisani;
3. The Christian Doctrine by Bellarmine;
4. The Manna of the Soul, by Segneri;
5. Compendium of Theology, by Charmes;
6. The Essence of Moral Theology, by Busembaum;
7. Month of Mary for Religious, by Pallotti.

Again we find ourselves in the presence of a little religious reference library, not specialized in character, but with an emphasis on the ascetical and the mystical. Pallotti's training in philosophy and theology was the best available at the time, the same training which produced so great a scholar, for instance, as Cardinal Wiseman. He possessed, as we have seen, a diploma of Professor of Greek and he had been awarded a doctor's degree in philosophy and theology, which was more than most of his contemporaries possessed. For ten years he was engaged in academic pursuits. Yet learning for its own sake, or professional teaching, even of the sacred sciences, was not his vocation.

There is an anecdote in Melia's "Life of Pallotti" which may provide us with a glimpse into his mind in this respect:

"The celebrated Abbé Chatôme sought and obtained an interview with Vincent in order to apprize him of a project contemplated by him of forming in France a union of priests for the higher theological studies only, without taking part in the ministry. Vincent thereupon answered him: 'It would be better to found a house of high virtues and of profound humility rather than one of high studies.'"

Not that Vincent was in any way opposed to profound studies for the clergy or anyone else. On the contrary, he inculcates in his rule that priests *must* engage in study, and that their efficiency depends on their proficiency, and so on. There was a famous Scripture Professor, whose name we have already mentioned — Don Giovanni Allemand, who consulted Vincent on the affairs of his soul. In a letter Vincent tells him:

"One can become a saint by cultivating literature, in the scientific academies, in the professorial chairs, in the circles of the erudite, no less than among the publicans and sinners of the world...."

What Vincent really wanted was that everything good in the world should be put to the service of religion. He felt that the Church in his generation needed more and more priests who would enter into contact with the souls to be saved and be able to convey goodness to them. As he told Allemand in another part of the letter just quoted: "You can become a saint by holding converse with everybody without distinction of persons, beginning your relationship with what interests them, but concluding with what interests you." Which, if your interest is sanctity, is a form of leading people to goodness. Should anyone therefore ask whether Pallotti encouraged any particular specialization among the clergy of his time and his Society the answer should be: yes, he wanted them to be specialized in making human contacts leading on to goodness, or sanctity. Is the need less urgent in our own day?

Although human sanctity is on another plane, it bears many resemblances to human suffering. Neither of them can be described with any sort of formula which sets up a true standard of measurement and there is a tremendous solitude about both of them. In the case of sanctity, the road which leads to union with God is as profoundly individual as the person who treads that road; there are, however, certain experiences which are generic to all the saints, and hence it is one of the most frequent things in the history of sanctity to find them seeking each other out. You never will find a friendless saint and you will find that among his friends there always were other saintly people. Who were the saintly persons in Pallotti's life?

There were many. In the first place, as is his due, we will mention St. Gaspar del Bufalo, whose career and achievements have been described in an earlier chapter. Then there was Bernard Clausi who was born in Calabria in Southern Italy in 1787, was ordained to the priesthood as a secular, then joined the Order of the Minims of St. Francis of Paola, one of the most rigorous orders in the Church, where perpetual abstinence is practiced in virtue of a solemn vow. His life was spent in the monasteries of his Order in various parts of Italy and on several occasions he was stationed in Rome. He acquired a great reputation for sanctity, for his power of performing prodigies and for predicting the future, and when it became known that he was resident in any particular place, the monastery was besieged with suppliants of all kinds and it was impossible for him to walk the streets without being followed by a concourse of people. So much so, that during one of his terms in Rome, the ecclesiastical authorities decided that it was best that Father Bernard should not go out of doors except in a closed carriage. There was in Rome a female branch of the Order of Minims where a very holy nun, the Venerable Luisa Maurizi, was spiritually directed by Vincent Pallotti. This convent was much visited by Father Bernard Clausi during his stay in Rome in 1830 and it seems to us likely that it was at this time that the two holy men became acquainted. We have related above the manner in which they took leave of each other on this earth. Then there was the Venerable Elizabeth Sanna, the strange pilgrim who came to Rome on her way to the Holy Land, and, hedged in by psychological barriers and perhaps inspired by some vision which is not easily comprehended, stayed in the Holy City till the end of her life. She was born in Sardinia in 1785 and from infancy was handicapped by the barbarous surgical treatment then in vogue as a cure for small-pox—the tendons of her forearms had been severed and she was unable to lift her hands as high as her face, could not comb her hair and in order to feed herself was forced to resort to a long-handled and unwieldy spoon. In spite of her handicap a husband was found for her and she married in 1808; there were five children and her husband died in 1825. She became a Franciscan tertiary and wore the habit around her house in the Sardinian village where she lived. Six years later she set out on a pilgrimage to the Holy Land, leaving her children in the care of relatives, one of whom was a priest; the ship in which she embarked took her to Genoa and she found it impossible, through lack of the necessary documents, to get another, so she decided to go to Rome and from there, when Providence provided an opportunity, to proceed to the Holy Land. Most of the journey from Genoa to Rome was done on foot, for she had very little money. She arrived in July, 1831, rented a little room in a house, now destroyed, near the Hostel of Santa Marta, within what are now the confines of the Vatican State. Here she stayed till she died. She was illiterate, knew no Italian when she came to Rome and learned it with difficulty and never perfectly; besides the handicap of her mutilated fore-arms she suffered from some affliction of the nerves of her neck and head which compelled her to keep her neck padded with a great wad of clothing. She was tiny, plain, sallow and bad-complexioned, with just one odd feature, which a witness in the Cause of her Beatification recalled long afterwards: she had intense black eyes, which appeared to look right into your soul. Most of her time was spent in and about the Basilica of St. Peter, where she heard Masses all morning. She lived on alms, which were unsought and she refused any sum greater than what she needed for that day.

She met Vincent Pallotti one day when she fol-lowed a procession from St. Peter's where she was on familiar ground, to the Pantheon, where she was lost. Because she spoke only the Sardinian dialect, she could not make anyone understand where she wanted to go. She met Vincent Pallotti and somehow he managed to make out what she wanted, and made her understand what she must do to get home. It was the beginning of an association which ended only in death. Elizabeth Sanna had heard about Pallotti but she was told that it was no use trying to go to con-fession to him because she would not be able to make herself understood. She persisted however, and finally Vincent became her spiritual director and he realized at once that here was someone strange and unusual, a soul whom God wished to walk in a special way. Perhaps he wanted to be sure, or perhaps he did not trust his understanding of her almost incomprehensible dialect; the fact is that he per-suaded her to find someone who understood her language and his, to whom she had to dictate some account of her manner of prayer. The documents are extant in the process of her beatification; couched in language of extreme simplicity one may read of a human soul moving through all the great degrees of prayer, from the vocal to the liturgical, a soul struggling to unshackle itself from some obstacle whose nature it does not understand but whose presence it knows. She had great gifts. People came to know that this poor illiterate beggarwoman had some insight which helped her to discern sincerity from falsehood and they began asking her advice; she seemed to know, sometimes at any rate, how things were going to turn out and her prayers were answered oftener than the prayers of anyone else within reach. People began approaching her in St. Peter's or going to her room. She was short, gruff and sometimes incommunicative. She did not always answer questions, but she always wanted the questioner to pray; if it was in her room, she would light candles in front of a picture of our Lady: *Virgo Potens*, and they would pray together. All sorts of people got to hear about her and visited her: a Duchess of Saxony, a prelate who later became a Cardinal, girls in search of husbands, wives fearful of losing their husbands, marchionesses, countesses, young women and young men who thought they had vocations, or that they hadn't.

Vincent Pallotti found in her an obedience which was heroic, and made it the basis of her sanctity. There was question of her returning to her family: a difficult and delicate matter, in which her feelings were deeply engaged. She left the matter in Vincent's hands and Vincent had her examined by a doctor, who declared that the long journey was out of the question. He taught her to place no value at all upon herself or upon anything which was not God; he made her, shy and awkward and most uncouth in

speech as she was, visit the hospitals every day
and give alms — she who lived on alms — to the poor
there, and above all to get them to pray. Some of them
laughed at her; others, seeing below the surface, took
her seriously. Slowly and patiently Vincent · taught
her new methods of prayer. Under his guidance
she made the three vows of the religious life.

Vincent learned in the course of their association
that Elizabeth Sanna's judgment was very sound
and he sometimes consulted her on the problems of
the Society. The advice of this peasant woman
who could neither read nor write was often wiser
than the counsel of learned men. She became devoted
to the Society as soon as it was founded, and very
earnestly, this woman who lived on charity, made
a will in its favor! The inheritance, when it came,
was better than rubies, for in accordance with that
will her body rests in the church of San Salvatore and
many prodigies have been wrought for those who have
gone there to pray by her tomb. Her picture, the
Virgo Potens, stands near by and many people have
found that our Lady delights to honor requests
made in that place before this image. "From the
time that the Society was founded until she died,"
one of her biographers says, "she lived for the Pallottines." In their material interests she was indefatigable; she stitched, she knitted, she sewed — with
her almost useless hands — and when the Society
was very poor she begged for it. "Our Society has two
great protectors," said the Rector General who
succeeded Pallotti, "one is a very poor woman,
Elizabeth Sanna, and the other is Cardinal Lambruschini."

These were the friends of Vincent Pallotti.
Reading over the details of their lives — some of them
very curious, as for instance the persecutions which
Clausi suffered at the hands of the devil, who attempted to push him down the stairs and once threw

him into the sea, and some people said that it was an attempt at suicide — one is struck by the intense and day-by-day sense of the supernatural in their human affairs. Their prayers were always being answered, in one way or another and the answers were always clear and distinct for their minds to grasp. There must have been a lot of people in that age and society who not only believed, but who were sure that they had seen as well.

We need not compare saint with saint, visionary with visionary, mystic with mystic. But this we feel we must say, that Vincent stands out in his age because he strove so intensely to implement his vision with the practical, rational means; the sort of things of which we are so fond in our own day, which sometimes, in our practicality, we confound with ends. How can faith be revived and charity spread throughout the world? One certain way, says Vincent Pallotti, is the institution and development of the Society of the Catholic Apostolate. How is the Church to be reformed? By means of a general council, he answers. How am I to overcome my rationalistic doubts against the truths of faith? asked Nicholas Wiseman. By helping the foreign missions, Vincent told him.

CHAPTER VII

Aspects of His Personality

In his physical characteristics, Vincent Pallotti was of lower middle stature, slight in figure and with a fairly prominent nose and a wide thin-lipped mouth. By the time of his death he had acquired a slight stoop and had lost most of his hair. He wore, according to the custom of the times, his hair long at the back; his ears were large as also were his hands, according to the evidence of the impressions which were taken after his death. He lived just before the age of photography and in consequence we are deprived of this means of determining his physical appearance. However, a death-mask was taken as he lay in his coffin and it remains the most valuable element for his iconography. Pictures and sketches were made of him at the same time, but it is not certain that any of them have survived; the earliest portraits in existence have a conventional quality about them which does not carry conviction as regards their objectivity. They do not strike the beholder as drawn from life.

We are more fortunate in the literary descriptions which have come down to us. The Abbé Gaume saw him in the flesh and placed on record the following literary portrait of Pallotti which was published in 1847:

"This extraordinary man is of small stature, thin and somewhat stooped. His hair is grey, his complexion pallid, his eyes large and blue like the Roman sky, his glance sweet and penetrating, his face oval and conveying a feeling of great purity, his manners are gentle and there is an air of melancholy and candor about his whole person, which, taken with his undoubting faith, inspires you with a cer tain feeling of filial confidence and religious respect which leaves you defenseless."

Another description is provided by the Abbé de Geslin de Kersolon, a French subdeacon who had been recommended in Loretto to make Pallotti's acquaintance; he subsequently joined the community.

"Pallotti was low-sized, somewhat stooped, quick in his movements, but not hasty; his gestures seemed to indicate that he considered life to be a brief affair and he was anxious not to lose a moment. His grey head was completely bald in front and allowed his ample forehead, beautiful and white as ivory, to be seen to the full. His features were fine and his dark eyes had a deep expression, which showed an extreme sweetness."

Pallotti was much attached to cleanliness and neatness; various anecdotes are told about his gentle manner of inculcating these virtues in his companions, by personally brushing the dust from their clothes, which they had neglected to cleanse after a journey, and so on. His own garments were often darned, but never ragged.

It does not appear that the solemnity and severity with which he conducted his inner life and the earnestness which colored his apostolic activity made him in any way sour and gloomy in his intercourse with others.

"He showed (says Melia) in the recreations at which he was sometimes present in a holy cheerfulness, so that he was a model and a rule for others how to make holy recreation. Moreover, the fecundity of his conceptions, the hilarity of his mind, the courtesy and sweetness of his manners, made it a real pleasure to be a partaker of his conversation. So that by his admirable behavior, Vincent made virtue amiable and a saintly life desirable."

His correspondence is full of examples of gentle courtesy, no matter what the quality of the person to whom he is writing; his refusals are made without harshness and with a certain aura of sincere regret; favors are asked with an engaging modesty but without subservience. Very frequently he introduces a request with a formula whose meaning is that here is an opportunity for that particular person to gain merit for himself and to please God.

One of the personal problems which must confront all men who are aspiring for heroic union with God, that is, sanctity, must be their adjustment to the people with whom they are surrounded. There is no one more conscious of his own unworthiness than the man who walks intimately with God and he must suffer very much when his contemporaries call him a saint to his face. To admit the attribution is to deny the truth about himself as he sees it. On the other hand, he knows that he is sincere in his aspirations, so that if any of his contemporaries suggests to him, or shouts after him in the street, that he is nothing but a hypocrite, he cannot, without doing an essential injury to himself and to God who is the object of his efforts, admit that the term is justified. What attitude must a man adopt when he is told to his face that he is a saint, or a hypocrite?

The difficulties arising from the adjustment which has to be made in the presence of such problems came upon Vincent very shortly after his ordination to the priesthood, as his Diary shows.

"If someone says to me: 'I am scandalizing you, aren't I?', I shall answer: 'Why? If you are afraid of scandalizing me, examine your actions, and if they are really scandalous, correct them, and if they are good, remember that it is written that the holy man must further sanctify himself, and the just man justify himself.

"If I am asked how I conduct myself in spiritual matters, I shall never answer regarding myself, except to my spiritual director, but rather I shall say how such and such a saint conducted himself in similar circumstances... and if I cannot think of any example from the saints, I will say: 'think how Jesus and Mary would have conducted themselves in these circumstances....'

"If someone says to me: 'So-and-so is a better person than you,' I will answer: 'I believe it; I have no doubt about it.'"

This matter of what today we would call human relations was in his thoughts even before his ordination to the priesthood, for as a seminarist he was already engaged in several enterprises which placed him in touch with various groups of people and he felt the need of establishing rules of conduct for himself.

"Vincent (he tells himself in his Diary) when you have to deal or communicate with anyone, consider that you are receiving a great honor...."

There is a special temptation which assails those who occupy positions of leadership; the urge to rectify the decisions made by others and to score them off with a show of greater knowledge and ability. Here is the rule of action which Vincent gave himself:

"Even when I am really able to decide and do things which others have not been able to decide or do, I shall not decide or do them unless this is required for the glory of God and the salvation of souls."

He also warns himself not to be in too much of a hurry:

"I will endeavor to arrange my work in such fashion that no carelessness shall arise from excessive haste."

The motivation behind these rules of conduct is not the mere construction of a balanced personality or the search for efficiency. Vincent is urging himself onwards from a high and pure motive of charity and religion.

"I will endeavor, in all my dealings with other beings, to act from the promptings of charity and obedience to the rule of what is more perfect; indeed, it is my intention always to do what is more perfect and more holy, and even when I am engaged in doing something which is of itself indifferent, I will endeavor to introduce a note of spirituality into the affair...."

As Vincent's spiritual personality gradually unfolded and developed, he arrived at a point where the defects and shortcomings of his own life, contrasted with the great mercies and graces which God was offering him, appeared so terrible in his eyes that he strove for complete detachment, distrust and contempt for his own unaided personality, which anyhow he held to be of no account. He compressed these sentiments into a formula: *nihil et peccatum* — "nothingness and sin," which appears in abbreviated form at the top of most of his letters. His insistence in using it in his correspondence is due, according to his biographer Melia, to his desire to humble himself before men, just as he was humbling himself before God. And whenever it happened that other people offended him in word or action, "he immediately asked to be excused," says Cardinal Lambruschini, "as though he had provoked them, although it was very far from the truth."

His manners and bearing were, as a matter of fact, those of a person who sought to live his life among his fellow-beings without attracting any attention whatever to himself. "Humble in his sweet, courteous and obliging manners," writes Melia, "humble in the way he held his head bent forward; humble in keeping his eyes cast down; humble in his walk and all his actions; humble in his clothing...; humble in saluting others and being always the first to uncover and bow to others...." He sought in fact to pass through life unnoticed. In his Diary we read this sentence:

"I desire to love God in this manner, that is to love Him without its being known to any but God, so that when

God calls me to dwell with Him in Heaven I may not be known any more but by Him."

Vincent Pallotti led an extraordinarily busy life. Callers poured in upon him, seeking recommendations, appealing for charitable assistance, consulting with him about the affairs of their spiritual life, applying for confession. His apostolate took him to a great many meetings and to reunions of sodalities; he conducted services for groups of people all over the city; nuns in enclosed convents called upon him to visit them in their monasteries to give them spiritual advice; he was constantly being summoned to attend the sick and the dying; for many years he had fixed assignments every week in the ecclesiastical colleges where he was spiritual director; he was responsible for the services in the church under his charge from the time he became Rector of the Church of the Holy Spirit. He was therefore on the move all the time and his routine was liable to be interrupted at any moment by some urgent appeal. He also had an extensive correspondence; almost two thousand letters written by him survived and it is reasonable to suppose that they are only a fraction of what he wrote. Correspondence replied to is correspondence read; and some of it was important correspondence; which required much meditation in order to give the correct reply. His letters alone were a heavy drain on his time.

Nevertheless, he somehow found means to get through an immense mass of writing of another type as well. It is known that much of his other writing was done at night and that some of it was done in a most uncomfortable position — on his knees.

"He had a fiery temperament," Cardinal Lambruschini, who knew him very well, has stated. But in his ordinary relationships he had so conquered this aspect of his personality that only a subtle mind could have discerned the lineaments of nature below those of grace. It is chiefly in his writings, which in many cases were not meant for other eyes than his own, that we can clearly discern the upsurgings and the impetuousness, the struggles and the vehemences of a soul which without witnesses of any kind, strives to express itself in the omniscient presence of God.

It is the writing of a man in a great hurry to express a great multitude of things which are in his heart, without any literary artifice whatever, with scarcely any preoccupation about the balance, the length or the concordances of the sentences. The ideas are set down, white-hot as they emerge into distinctness in his mind; patterns of expression keep repeating themselves over and over again because in their literary expression they are merely the registration of an interior habit of thought. Thus the thought of "infinity" or "eternity" arising in prayer led him into the formulation of a cycle, frequently repeated, of aspirations in which his mind strove to equate itself with these conceptions in order to utilize them in that limitless adoration of God to which he felt impelled.

A distinction must be made, however, between what he wrote for publication, what he wrote for the instruction or edification of others, even though not intended for publication, and what he wrote for himself alone. In the year 1833 he prepared and published anonymously three Manuals for the devout celebration of the month of Mary, a devotion which had not yet come into general use in Rome. The first of these Manuals he designed for use in monasteries and religious houses. The second is prepared for the use of the ecclesiastics and seminarians and it was employed during the month of May at evening devotions for the clergy, carried out for many years, first at the Church of the Holy Spirit, and later at San Salvatore. The third Manual is drawn up for the use of the laity. During his lifetime this was reprinted several times, editions being made of it in Genoa and Turin as well as in Rome. After his death it was repeatedly republished by the Society of the Catholic Apostolate.

Vincent is the author of a commentary on the First Article of the Creed, in the form of thirty-one meditations, which he entitled: God, Infinite Love. This work is based on profound theological knowledge and develops in orderly fashion the doctrine of the soul of man as the image of God. His discussion ranges from the natural to the supernatural order and each one of the divine attributes becomes the object of a special meditation, whose purpose is to demonstrate that every man must endeavor to establish and increase within his soul the image of these majestic attributes of the Divinity. This work was not published during his lifetime and its design shows that it was part of a projected larger work.

He likewise prepared for publication an account of the last days and death of a cleric in 1843, whom Vincent attended during the last days of his life. The events surrounding the death of this cleric were the object of much comment and discussion in Rome at the time and in order to avoid adding fuel to the fire, Vincent decided not to print the pamphlet which he had prepared. It was, however, printed many years later in the collected edition of his works.

On the advice of his spiritual director, he got ready for publication a Memoir of Don Carlo Torlonia, of the ducal family of that name. The document was ready for printing in 1848 but the revolutionary events of that year delayed publication till long after Vincent's death. There is also a short Memoir of Giovanni Allemand, the Professor of Scripture who has been mentioned before; it was circulated among friends in manuscript form.

Also extant are the Depositions made by Vincent in the Causes of Beatification of the Venerable Luisa Maurizi and St. Gaspar del Bufalo, both of them lengthy documents, which have since been printed in the Acts of the respective Processes.

Several statements drawn up at various times explanatory of the nature and the purpose of the Society of the Catholic Apostolate were prepared by Vincent, as if for publication, but were not printed during his lifetime, on account of the controversy which had sprung up around the title of the Society. A similar fate befell the first "Rule of the Pious Society of the Catholic Apostolate" which he compiled in 1839. His other rule, the "Rule of the Congregation of the Catholic Apostolate" which was intended for the central, clerical body which sustains and supports the Pious Society, was still under revision at the time of his death. A short condensation of this rule, which is known as "The Thirty-Three Points" because it is divided into that number of sections, in honor of the years of our Lord's life, was also composed by Vincent; it was printed after his death and has several times been published for the edification of his followers.

The various memoirs from his pen are composed with great attention to exactitude in historical detail and are written in an agreeable and easy style, betraying the presence of a scholarly and cultivated mind. The writings devoted to the explanation of the Catholic Apostolate are carefully planned statements, closely reasoned, the arguments being put forward with force and at the same time with modesty and amiability.

There is one characteristic which is common to all his writings, whatever their immediate purpose and that is that they are all unmistakably directed towards God. Here is a man who takes his pen in his hand and everything that he has to say is said in relation to the Divinity. Nothing is said for its own sake, or for the sole sake of the subject which is being dealt with. The writer is not concerned to display talent or make a show of erudition or make use of eloquence for its own sake; or to search around for the arresting metaphor or the striking comparison; or to construct elegant figures of speech. The writer's work is purely instrumental.

Vincent Pallotti's edited correspondence is the correspondence of a man who has no time to waste. As a rule each letter deals with one subject, and when several are dealt with, the topics are sometimes numbered. They give the sensation of letters written in haste, but none of them, so to speak, are hasty and there is a uniform sweetness of expression about them. "I venture to explain to you," "I take the liberty of presenting to you," "I ask you to have the charity," "I am anxious for you to have the merit of the following good deed"—they are all gracious little documents and one can imagine the recipients keeping them not only because of the writer, but because of the intrinsic beauty of the gentle sentiments which are portrayed in them.

A considerable proportion of his letters are given over in supplementary spiritual direction; encouragement to people to follow up advice already given; explanations of counsels, warnings against pitfalls, incitements to greater progress and so on.

There is a great patience in his correspondence. One hundred and fifty of them are addressed to a single person: a scrupulous priest attached to the papal service abroad, who needs to be reassured about each practical detail of his life. Thirty more are sent to a certain decayed nobleman who constantly bewails his sad lot and keeps importuning Pallotti to advance the interests of his sons, which Vincent, to the best of his power, does, but the Count is never satisfied and he wanders back and forth between his own woes and the needs of his family. Perhaps there is a note of unconscious humor in Pallotti's constant recommendation to this good mournful man that he must cultivate patience—which he was unquestionably helping Vincent himself to do.

Then there is the Mother Abbess who for love of humility wishes to resign her post and become a lay-sister in another convent. Vincent loved humility, but he knew about the subtler forms of pride, too, so he writes:

"Your idea of going to another monastery as a lay-sister will not supply for your unworthiness, because the condition of a lay-sister is too high and sublime a state for you. Give up this idea, and bear in mind that in your religious life, there should be more work than speech; hence, few words and many deeds; good deeds and well done."

There was a religious brother who felt inclined to leave his community and enter another where he could become a priest; this in spite of sound advice to the contrary. He applies to Vincent for approval of the step he intends to take, and Vincent discourages him categorically: "Be content with the state you are in; do not look for another Institute but make the best of the one you are in." And then he touches the nerve of the matter with these words: "Docility, docility, docility." Frank and salutary letters; so the recipients must have thought, for they kept them for many years and then handed them over for the Process.

His letters are all purposeful and there is no hint in them that they, or any part of them, were written for relaxation or for the intellectual pleasure of disclosing his mind. During the latter part of his life he wrote a large number of letters to his earliest follower, Melia, who was living in London, and in them we find the nearest approach to correspondence being used for communication of news; but even then it is news about the religious activities of the brethren, their comings and goings on missions, their health, their safety during the revolution, the vicissitudes of the revolution itself insofar as it affected the community, and so on. And even then the flow of information is interrupted every now and again with exhortations and spiritual counsels, as though the writer felt that the trivial must be balanced with what is really important.

The members of Vincent's community never doubted that one day he would be placed on the altars of the Catholic Church and they determined that his room and its furniture should be kept exactly as it was when he died and all his effects assembled, catalogued and stored. It is possible, therefore, to go back a century, when visiting this room and get the feeling of Pallotti's age and day, by surveying this poor room and the pathetic—and somewhat terrifying—objects which have been preserved.

This was already an old house when the Society of the Catholic Apostolate took it over in 1845. Old and small, as a Latin inscription set in the wall of a long corridor which runs parallel to the little church, recalls:

"...parva domus
Summos Pontifices Xystos edidit ista duos."

"This little house produced the two Popes Sixtus." They were the fourth and fifth of that name, former Procurators-General of the Conventual Franciscan Order, for this house was for centuries the residence of that official of the Order. It is known too that St. Philip Neri dwelt here for a while, and another saint, the Conventual Franciscan St. James della Marca. This small old house is built around the apse of the church and access to it was obtained by a long corridor running along the side of the church. It was a three-story building and between the second and third story some forgotten architect constructed a room which opens off a turn in the stairs—a sort of mezzanine. Access to the room is gained by a small doorway with wooden jambs, and on the door is a little oblong frame enclosing a sheet of paper on which is written, in Vincent's hand, a list of places: church, sacristy, library, out-of-doors; opposite each place on the list there is a little hole in the wood and hanging from the top of the frame, on a piece of string, is a small pin: the usual method employed in religious houses to let callers know where the inmate of a room is to be found at any given time. The room itself is long, narrow and oblong, divided into two spaces by an archway which projects a couple of feet into the room; if a curtain were hung on this archway one can visualize a little bedroom and a sitting room. The architecture of the place is clearly determined by the proximity of the staircase and the archway mentioned would appear to be a structural feature demanded by the thrust of the stairs.

The floor of the room, which has a window looking to a yard, is of roughly glazed brick. The outer chamber contains a little eighteenth-century writing desk rather pleasantly inlaid. Vincent is known to have used it when he lived at the Church of the Holy Spirit and he may have brought it there from his home; it is, perhaps, a family piece. Some pictures hang on the wall, among them a pencil sketch of Peter Paul Pallotti, made, some say, by Vincent himself: under it he has written: "My excellent Father."

The second chamber contains a small bookcase, in which he kept the books he needed most frequently; others were stored in the community Library. Next to the bookcase is a large kneeling desk, with lockers on both sides and ledges on which the arms could rest. The kneeler has a high wooden back and is about five feet high and on both sides the lockers are carried, and in the center, above the kneeling space, there is set in the recess a Calvary, with the background painted in vivid colors. Vincent is known to have painted this himself and to have applied their present coat of paint to the figures on the Calvary, for he had some skill in these arts. In the corner of the room opposite the kneeling desk is a high wooden bed, rather narrow, of the type still seen in the homes of the very poor in the Italian countryside. It is covered with a thick rough coverlet. On the wall over the bed hangs a large lithographed card, with the portrait of a saint for each day in the year. Several other pictures are around the walls, and on a little pedestal, a statue of our Lord.

In a large room nearby in the Pallotti Museum are kept his personal possessions; a clerical hat with a very broad brim, three-cornered and with the leaf curved after the napoleonic fashion — the usual clerical hat of the period; an umbrella, a pair of gloves, a watch, a very much worn-down razor, strop and hone, a knife, fork, spoon and drinking vessel of poor quality. In another case are to be seen his inkwell and pen, samples of his correspondence, the notebooks he filled with his minute writing, all the letters firmly formed, with no scrawls and no trailing. And in another case are his instruments of penance, three rusty disciplines with wooden handles to which are attached little steel chains ending in spikes, two little whips of rawhide thongs, two sticks, a form of hair shirt and a length of iron chain.

In another case hangs his habit, made of rough serge and his girdle, after the fashion of the community which he founded; some sacerdotal vestments, a missal, two chalices; the Capuchin habit in which he slept each night for many years; a large cloak for street wear; his shoes, very worn and of poor material.

There is a certain neatness about the collection, which glows with an aura of poverty beyond and above the intrinsic character of the objects themselves. You feel somehow that the person who used these things chose them because he wanted to be poor, not only in spirit but in the hard fact. These poor little things were themselves serving Poverty.

But the case of instruments of penance is something else. Here is an evidential contact with an older world; a reference to a time when the mass of mankind did not doubt that the body of man had to be brought into subjection to the spirit and that the ancient wisdom laid down there was one excellent way of doing it — if God inspired you to use this means and your spiritual advisers allowed that the inspiration was valid. We are inclined to shudder at these evidences of self-inflicted physical pain, we people of this generation which is responsible, in one way or another, for inflicting more physical pain on other men than any generation of mankind since the world began. Perhaps if there were more disciplines, more hair shirts used in secret, there would be fewer concentration camps and torture chambers in their world.

One looks at these things in the Pallotti Museum and wonders: who ever made them and where did they come from? Surely there never was a time in the world when someone made a living from the manufacture of these unusual objects; surely there never was a time when some religious object shop, some repository, added as a subtitle: "Instruments of penance sold here"? No, these things were born in some obscure monastery, from the anonymous hands of some artisan turned monk who was skilled in the use of steel and leather. Perhaps there were bequeathed by one anonymous penitent to another, penitential legacies more treasured than silver or gold. Perhaps we are looking at things which for centuries passed from the hands of one Camaldolese hermit to another, nameless and secret, until at last they came before the eyes of men when Vincent Pallotti died and left them behind him. Now they have come into the light of another day, after many holy hands were laid upon them. Here they lie now, converted into statements; having acquired another purpose from the single one for which they are made statements mutely testifying to the sanctity of the last hands which used them; statements informing us who view them, that God has His own ways of leading to Himself those who wish to love Him.

Vincent Pallotti's great dream of generously infusing new life into the Catholic organizations by bringing them closer together, so that from unity strength might be generated had always seemed utopian to many people, who during his lifetime could not but venerate the man and admire his transparent sanctity. At the time of his death only a dozen priests, all told, had joined the inner nucleus of his Society: too few, it seemed, to attempt so vast a work as Vincent planned. There was as well the disputed title of his organization "the Society of the Catholic Apostolate," which had been so resisted in the beginning; which, while Pallotti lived, was allowed to subsist on sufferance, in homage to the great prestige of the Founder. God called him away and people began to speculate what would happen now; would the few faithful disciples keep together, or would they melt away like snow before the sun? They were very few, they were very poor and they had loads of work if they were going to keep up to the high and exacting standards set by the Founder; a heavier burden even than before, really, if they were to attempt to shoulder, even in part, the work which he personally used to perform.

These were not favorable times for the Catholic religion in the Latin world. More than one historian, reviewing the nineteenth century, has pointed out that during this span of time the influence of the Church receded like a great tide in its ancient strongholds in Europe: France, Spain, Italy, and in Latin America, whereas it advanced in the Anglo-Saxon countries and their colonies. The tide receded strongly even in the Papal States, where the unsolved political question kept providing the enemies of the Papacy with a continuing reason for working to bring down the temporal rule of the Popes by turning their subjects against religion as such. For twenty years after the death of Pallotti, from 1850 till the crash came in 1870, the Sovereign Pontiff ruled uneasily and many clear-thinking people realized that the sands were running out. It was not a good time for the infant Society of the Catholic Apostolate to develop.

Add to this the question of the title. Now that Pallotti was gone, the Society had only one powerful friend left—Cardinal Lambruschini, who had been Gregory XVI's secretary of state. In 1854 the Cardinal died and a few weeks later the title of the institute was changed to that of "Pious Society of Missions," which it was to bear for almost a century. In 1947 by a gracious act of the Holy See, the original title was restored, for its true significance had by then been made very clear because of the similar designations which had in the meantime been adopted by other organizations which had since come into existence.

Pallotti's companions did not however lose heart. They met after his death and elected one of their number to take his place—a man of great talent and virtue named Vaccari. This man deserves a remembrance from all Catholics, for, as far as we know, he was the first to petition and obtain from the Holy See that the invocation "Blessed be the Immaculate Conception" be added to the Divine Praises after Benediction of the Blessed Sacrament. But Vaccari did not live long and after his death the Society reached nadir. There were problems arising from the scarcity of personnel, problems about the rules of the corporate society which Pallotti had not had time to complete before his death. The surviving companions, who had seen the vision through Vincent's eyes were resolute men, who were held up by difficulties but were not broken by them. The turning point came when Fr. Faa di Bruno took the helm in 1869 and proceeded to build a great missionary college in Northern Italy and to develop the languishing studentate in Rome itself. The Society began to emerge from its winter; it is worthy of note that the change came just when this College of Foreign Missions was established. Pallotti had longed for such a College and several times had been on the point of putting it into execution, but each time some unforeseen obstacle prevented it. He himself felt that this opposition came in reality from "the enemy of all goodness," as he phrased it, for he held that the devil has a special hatred for foreign missions, as he warned Wiseman when he heard that the latter was considering the foundation of a foreign missionary college in England in the year 1849. Now at last Pallotti's wish was accomplished and missionaries were to go forth to the ends of the world, and they were to be men wearing the habit he had selected, living according to the principles he had laid down.

The flow of manpower led to a considerable development of the Society of the Catholic Apostolate which spread into the Americas (USA 1884), Brazil, Uruguay, Argentina (1886), Germany (1891), and many other countries. Missions were developed in West Africa, among the aboriginal Australians, in East and South Africa and in India; the process is in full flower. The consciousness of the Society's mission of a universal coordinated apostolate has likewise been growing. The Society has done its share in bearing the burdens of the Church, the labor of the day and the heat, wherever her priests and religious have been called.

The Pallottian ideal for consecrated sisterhoods has also taken firm root in many countries. These sisterhoods, which have come into existence either as branches of the parent stem which was planted by Pallotti himself, or have grown out of his ideals as preached and taught by his followers, are working in the mission fields in many parts of the world, in the hospitals and the schools and among the poor.

Vincent's companions never forgot that at the back of his great vision, supporting and giving it reality, was the principle that the clergy were to unite, each without sacrificing the specific character of its Order, in the apostolate, and that this Society must be forever dedicated to the task of enlisting the laity in the hierarchical apostolate of the Church. The idea may have seemed revolutionary when he preached it in the early nineteenth century for did it not sound as though he wished to suppress the barriers which must divide clergy from laity? But time has shown that there are not two kinds of Catholics, clerical Catholics and lay Catholics, but just one sort of Catholic, though each man's function in the Church may be different from the other's. That is what Vincent meant when he asked that laity and clergy must engage in a charitable rivalry as to who may do more, each in his own place, for the good of religion. And that is what Pius XI meant when he declared that Vincent is the forerunner of modern Catholic Action, which he defined as the participation of the laity in the hierarchical apostolate of the Church. Vincent's companions and their successors did not cease to co-opt people, laity and clergy, into the Association or Pious Union which Pallotti left them as a precious legacy at the time of his death. And in one form or another, the Association continues to do its work in all parts of the world where there are Pallottines, who share the spiritual treasures which successive Popes have bestowed on the organization, and on those who cooperate with St. Vincent Pallotti's Society of the Catholic Apostolate.

Epilogue

The first official step for Vincent's canonization was taken in Rome two years after his death. This consisted in the opening of what is known as the Diocesan Process, that is, the preliminary investigation which is made by the bishop of the diocese where the candidate has lived.

The next step is the introduction of the Cause before the officials of the Congregation of Rites in Rome, which takes cognizance of all the information collected in the course of the Diocesan Process and decides whether the matter should be proceeded with. In Vincent's case, this was done in the year 1887.

The writings of the candidates are then examined and approved if their quality is such as to deserve this approval. In Vincent's case, the approval was granted in 1895.

In 1906 the tomb where his remains were resting was opened, the seals removed from the coffin and the body examined — a verification demanded by the Process of Beatification. The body, resealed in a new coffin, was then restored to its place in the tomb.

In 1932 the late Pope Pius XI promulgated the Decree certifying that Vincent during his lifetime had possessed and practiced the Christian virtues to a heroic degree.

In 1950 Vincent was declared Blessed. His remains were taken from their resting-place, enclosed in a sarcophagus of bronze and crystal, and placed beneath the High Altar of the Church of San Salvador. The visitor and pilgrim may venerate them in this place.

And now this humble holy man, who wished to be forgotten, has been raised to the highest honor to man. His name has been placed on the Canon of the Saints and his path to sanctity has been held up as a model and an example to all men.

Vincent Pallotti's Society of the Catholic Apostolate has fulfilled his death-bed prophecy that it would live and would be blessed by God. At the present time there are two thousand five hundred members of the priestly branch of the Society.

The Sisterhoods of the Catholic Apostolate — they are four in number and two of them stem back to Pallottian times — are engaged in missionary teaching and hospital work in various parts of the world. There are more than one thousand five hundred sisters.

Pallotti's great dream of a worldwide apostolic movement has come true in other ways besides the concrete achievement of his Society of the Catholic Apostolate. His basic idea that the laity must be made conscious of their responsibility and that they must be organized for the apostolate, that idea which seemed so revolutionary and questionable when he first propounded it, is now accepted as a matter of course. When Pius XI defined Catholic Action as "the participation of the laity in the hierarchical apostolate of the Church," he was formulating the essence of Pallotti's idea. And the great Pope paid homage to Vincent's lonely and unrewarded struggle when he declared that Pallotti was the Precursor of Catholic Action, who divined not only its essence, but also its very name. The Pontiff, Pope John XXIII, in his address to the Congress of Spiritual Directors, on September 9, 1962, corroborated the judgment of his predecessor in these terms: "The foundation of the Society of the Catholic Apostolate was the starting-point in Rome of Catholic Action as we know it today."

Pallotti's second ideal, that the barrier of separation between regular and secular clergy, which he considered one of the chief evils of his time, should be broken down and that "rivalry in charity" should be substituted for it, has likewise transcended the limits of his Society and has become today a dominant theme in the Church as a whole. "During the last forty years," Pope John XXIII declared in an Allocution to the religious superiors of Italy on November 15, 1960, "Our predecessors have repeatedly expressed their wish for synchronized and converging apostolic action, which should be free from useless and damaging lack of agreement based on the pretext of mutually exclusive fields of labor, or worse still, on a species of intolerance of the good work performed by others in the same field. According to the mind of the Supreme Pontiffs, true collaboration must be founded on the cooperation of secular and regular clergy in the diocese working together harmoniously under the direction of the bishop."

Similarly, Pallotti's missionary ideal is today shared by the Church in every land, and it is impelled forward by the same sense of urgency which drove him onwards all his life. "Caritas Christi urget nos" — the charity of Christ urges us on — was the motto which he inscribed on the seal of his Society; Christ's charity for the dwellers in darkness has indeed urged many of his most faithful followers to cross the oceans to these other children of God.

From his place near God's bright throne, St. Vincent Pallotti looks down and blesses us all — his spiritual children, the men and women of the Catholic Apostolate, who in various ways are associated with it and have shared in the riches of his spirit; and those whom Providence has inspired to live and die dedicated to the same high purposes which led him all his life and which are still dear to him in the place of his heavenly reward.

SAINTS

Autobiography of St. John Neumann, C.SS.R.

Translation, Introduction, Commentary and Epilogue by Alfred C. Rush, CSSR

"This autobiography is important for the insight it gives us into the character of Bishop Neumann, of Philadelphia, into Neumann as a person...how he faced life, how he coped with difficulties, disappointments and setbacks....

"The life of John Neumann remains a challenge to all of us...to manifest to all the world our loyalty to Jesus Christ and His Church." —John Cardinal Krol
118 pages
cloth $3.50; paper $2.50 — ST0010

Breviary Lives of the Saints

Rev. Frederick J. Murphy, MA, STL

Two volumes (I: September to January; II: February to May). Latin selections with commentary and a vocabulary. Each of these two volumes will satisfy a semester language requirement in Latin and at the same time be a vehicle for classroom learning and appreciation of the history and tradition of the Church.

Vol. I: September to January; 328 pages; available in paper only $2.50 — ST0020

Vol. II: February to May; 310 pages; available in cloth only $3.50 — ST0030

A translation for student use. (Vol. I-II) $1.00 — ST0031

Doctor Luke, Beloved Physician

Msgr. Leo Gregory Fink

A vibrant presentation of the Christ-like personality of the great physician of early Christian times. 216 pages
cloth $4.00; paper $2.75 — ST0040

Every Man My Brother

Francis Sweeney, SJ

The colorful life of Bernardine Realino, who dramatically abandoned a career of law and politics in Renaissance Italy to become a Jesuit, a minister of God's mercy and a saint. 178 pages
cloth $4.00; paper $3.00 — ST0049

Every Man's Challenge

Daughters of St. Paul

The warm and dynamic personalities of 38 saints are captured in brief inspiring profiles. Their lives confirm Christ's message: sanctity is "everyman's challenge."
345 pages
cloth $5.00 — ST0050

Families That Followed the Lord

Martin P. Harney, SJ

This book contains the lives of over one hundred fifty brother and sister saints of various nationalities, places, and times. This account of fraternal and religious loyalty, which blends the best of what is human and divine, cannot fail to touch and inspire the reader of today. 145 145 pages
cloth $3.95; paper $2.95 — ST0060

Hands for Others

Sister Louis Passero, FMA

Mary Mazzarello, a peasant woman of our times, though handicapped by poverty and little learning, founds a religious congregation, the Salesians, dedicated to teaching, nursing and social works of the Church. A compelling biography of a woman of great hope. 80 pages

Magister paperback 75¢ — ST0070

Heavenly Friends, A Saint for Each Day

Rosalie Marie Levy

A superb book, epitomizing the lives of more than 400 famous saints. 486 pages

deluxe $8.00; cloth or plastic $6.00; paper $5.00 — ST0080

In Garments All Red

Godfrey Poage, CP

The life of St. Maria Goretti, a shining example of teenage heroism. This young Italian girl from a peasant family preferred death rather than sin against purity. 119 pages

cloth $3.00; paper $1.50 — ST0090

Joseph, the Just Man

Rosalie Marie Levy

A complete biography, supplemented with accounts of favors granted and selections of special prayers. 285 pages

cloth $4.00; paper $3.00 — ST0100

Joseph: The Man Closest to Jesus

Francis L. Filas, SJ

Never before has all this wealth of intensely interesting and little-known facts about St. Joseph been compiled into a single book. This can truly be called a "little Summa" of St. Joseph, as the only survey existing in any language of the complete life, theology, and devotional history of St. Joseph. 682 pages

cloth $7.75; paper $6.50 — ST0110

The Legacy of St. Patrick

Martin P. Harney, SJ

The legacy of St. Patrick, which he would bequeath to his brethren and their descendants, was his own holy idealism. It can be found in his two writings, the Confession of St. Patrick and the Letters to the Soldiers of Coroticus.

A thoughtful perusal of the Confession and of the Letter will reward the reader with a true and an intimate knowledge of St. Patrick. 148 pages

cloth $3.50; paper $2.25 — ST0120

The Little Bishop
Episodes in the Life of St. John Neumann, CSSR

Paschal Turbet, CSSR

Human but faith-filled incidents from the life of St. John Neumann—priest, missionary, bishop—the man of prayer and action who toiled for the Church and all God's people in the strife-torn years of 19th century America. 148 pages

cloth $3.50; paper $2.50 — ST0130

Magnificent Witnesses

Martin P. Harney, SJ

Simple, heart-warming, soul-stirring sketches of the English and Welsh martyrs, canonized by Pope Paul VI on October 25, 1970. The martyrs included 13 secular priests, 20 religious (of 5 orders), 4 laymen and 3 laywomen. All gave their lives for the fundamental doctrine of the Primacy of the Pope. 80 pages

cloth $2.50; paper $1.50 — ST0140

The Man in Chains, St. Paul

Rosalie Marie Levy

An intriguing life of one of the world's greatest heroes and saints—the Apostle Paul.
225 pages
cloth $4.00; paper $3.00 — ST0150

Moments of Decision

Daughters of St. Paul

Profiles of 28 saints from many backgrounds and states in life. Portrayed with warmth and vitality, their lives teach us to use our "moments of decision" for Christ and His people. 315 pages
cloth $5.00; paper $4.00 — ST0170

Mother Cabrini

Daughters of St. Paul

Animated story of the labors of the first American-citizen saint, whose greatest happiness lay in caring for the orphans, the sick and the destitute, and saving souls in a new land. 223 pages
cloth $3.50; paper $2.50 — ST0180

Mother Seton—wife, mother, educator, foundress, saint

Daughters of St. Paul

This fast-paced life of "an authentic daughter of America" (Pope John's term) is completed by selections from Mother Seton's own writings—Spiritual Gems—that permit us to glimpse the deep spirituality of the first American-born saint. 140 pages
cloth $3.95 — ST0160

Saint and Thought for Everyday

Profiles by Daughters of St. Paul
Thoughts by Rev. James Alberione, SSP, STD

Brief sketches of lives of the saints for all year are presented according to the new calendar of saints.

Challenging daily thoughts by the renowned author Fr. James Alberione are arranged so as to assist us in our growth to full stature in Christ. 311 pages
cloth $3.95 — ST0190

Saint of the Impossible

Daughters of St. Paul

Fast-paced chapters tell of St. Rita's childhood and youth, of her will to succeed in her stormy marriage, of the transformation worked in her husband by her prayer and suffering for him, of her two sons, their death and her widowed loneliness. Even St. Rita's desire for religious life was thwarted at first, but the belief in God's unfailing care never left her...and she succeeded.
104 pages
cloth $3.95 — ST0290

Saints for the Modern Woman

Rev. Luke Farley

This book brings to the fore the modern woman's very real call to holiness by introducing her to some of her feminine predecessors in sanctity—women like herself from every century and walk of life. 264 pages
cloth $4.75; paper $3.50 — ST0360

Saint Anthony of Padua The Life of the Wonder-Worker

Isidore O'Brien, OFM

Flaming charity, unflagging zeal, unique power as preacher and teacher of the Faith—these qualities combine to make St. Anthony a powerful wonder-worker and intercessor on our behalf.
174 pages

cloth $5.00; paper $4.00 — ST0200

St. Bernard of Clairvaux

Msgr. Leon Cristiani

Bernard influenced the 12th century as no other monk did. But our interest is especially focused on what went on inside of him, within his soul, in his cloistered and hidden life, his life of prayer and penance, his life of union with God, in a word, in his religious and mystical life.

172 pages
cloth $3.95; paper $2.95 — ST0210

St. Catherine of Siena

Igino Giordani

The 14th century was one of the most turbulent in the history of Christianity. A semi-literate Italian woman dominated that century with her prodigious temporal activity. Readers are deeply led into the recesses of Catherine's mysticism— an outstanding life of a recently proclaimed Doctor of the Church.

258 pages
cloth $5.95 — ST0220

St. Francis de Sales and His Friends

Maurice Henry-Couannier

In selecting the most significant features of his life the author has discovered that St. Fràncis is probably best understood through his friends and friendships and against the background of the people he knew and loved, for in a very special way he deserves to be called the Saint of Friendship.

414 pages
cloth $5.00 — ST0230

St. Francis of Assisi

Msgr. Leon Cristiani

Msgr. Leon Cristiani's life of St. Francis offers the reader facts, authentic traditions, revered texts and a hope to foster in the reader a deep love and admiration for the saint whose fruitful life he tells. 164 pages
cloth $4.95 — ST0240

St. Gemma, the Passion Flower

Msgr. Joseph Bardi

An extraordinary story of a young woman whose intense love for Jesus Christ became incarnate through an exceptional gift of God—the stigmata, the very wounds of Christ. 182 pages
cloth $3.50 — ST0250

St. Joan of Arc, Virgin— Soldier

Msgr. Leon Cristiani

The author scrupulously strives to present the simple, naked, historical truth about the life and times of Joan of Arc. He also outlines the supernatural in Joan's life in all its clarity.

160 pages
cloth $3.95; paper $2.95 — ST0260

St. Margaret Mary Alacoque

Msgr. Leon Cristiani

An unforgettable biography of the great apostle and missionary of the Sacred Heart. Drawing from her own writings, we relive the drama of the "great revelations" which were to cause repercussions throughout the Christian world. 156 pages
cloth $5.00; paper $4.00 — ST0270

St. Martin de Porres

Richard Cardinal Cushing

For forty-five years St. Martin dedicated himself almost entirely to the performance of spiritual and corporal works of mercy. "A thumb-nail sketch in which the 'digitus Dei' clearly appears in the life and work of St. Martin."

"Central California Register"
80 pages
cloth $2.50; paper $1.25 — ST0280

St. Patrick and the Irish

Richard Cardinal Cushing

An absorbing biography of a great conqueror for Christ and his saintly followers, including Columbanus, Bridget and Brendan. 144 pages

cloth $3.50; paper $2.00 — ST0300

St. Paul, Apostle and Martyr

Igino Giordani

By a happy choice the author has built his simple, direct and scholarly picture upon this word: Apostle—an excellent account of the infant Church—enhanced also by a pictorial biography of Paul done in famous art masters and two sections of stimulating photos. 38 full-color illustrations and 33 in black and white. 392 pages

cloth $7.00; paper $6.00 — ST0310

St. Pius X, Pope

Most Rev. Jan Olav Smit

Journey through the boyhood, priesthood, papacy and sainthood of this remarkable man— warm, lovable, humorous— capable of leading the people of God with extraordinary wisdom— the influence of which we still feel in the Church today. 184 pages

cloth $4.00; paper $3.00 — ST0320

St. Teresa of Avila

Giorgio Papasogli

It took the author a year's visit to Spain, exhaustive research and an intensive study of all the existing material before he was ready to write. The result was an entirely new biography of one of the most written-about women in the world. 410 pages

cloth $5.00 — ST0330

St. Theresa, the Little Flower

Sister Gesualda of the Holy Spirit

The story of this young Carmelite nun has won worldwide fame. Read her simple way of love and perfection—her efficacious key to sanctity. Thousands of souls have received favors through the intercession of this "Patroness of the Missions" who promised to shower petals of roses on everyone. 270 pages

cloth $4.95 — ST0340

St. Vincent de Paul

Msgr. Leon Cristiani

Known as the "saint of charity," and founder of several religious congregations, Vincent de Paul is portrayed in these pages as the father of the poor. All will feel inclined to pray to this great saint and to imitate him who burned with the love of Christ and his neighbor. 170 pages

cloth $3.95; paper $2.95 — ST0350

Son of the Passion

Godfrey Poage, CP

A popular teenage boy, Gabriel Possenti entered the Passionist Order and achieved sainthood . . . *not* by doing *extraordinary* things —but by doing *ordinary* things extraordinarily well! 120 pages

cloth $3.50; paper $2.25 — ST0370

The Story of Monica and Her Son Augustine

Msgr. Leon Cristiani

The stirring story of a woman's faith and steadfastness in prayer that won the conversion of her wayward son. 176 pages

cloth $3.95; paper $2.95 — ST0380

Three Ways of Love

Frances Parkinson Keyes

The world-famous author here captures the romance, the

tragedy and the history of three great women: St. Agnes, whose name has become synonymous with courage; St. Frances of Rome, a mother and the protectress of the poor and sick; and St. Catherine of Siena, the famous ambassadress and stateswoman. 304 pages
cloth $6.00; paper $5.00 — ST0390

The Village Priest Who Fought God's Battles
St. John Mary Vianney
Msgr. Leon Cristiani

The lovable Cure of Ars, patron of all diocesan priests, is widely known for his battles with the devil and his victory over the power of evil. Here he comes alive in his ministry of prayer, penance and apostolic zeal. But first we meet the man who fought his own spiritual battles—a great source of inspiration and courage in our own war against evil.
172 pages
cloth $4.00; paper $3.00 — ST0400

Please order from any of the addresses at the end of this book, specifying title and item number.

Daughters of St. Paul

IN MASSACHUSETTS
  50 St. Paul's Ave. Jamaica Plain, Boston, MA 02130;
    617-522-8911; 617-522-0875;
  172 Tremont Street, Boston, MA 02111; **617-426-5464;**
    617-426-4230
IN NEW YORK
  78 Fort Place, Staten Island, NY 10301; **212-447-5071**
  59 East 43rd Street, New York, NY 10017; **212-986-7580**
  7 State Street, New York, NY 10004; **212-447-5071**
  625 East 187th Street, Bronx, NY 10458; **212-584-0440**
  525 Main Street, Buffalo, NY 14203; **716-847-6044**
IN NEW JERSEY
  Hudson Mall — Route 440 and Communipaw Ave.,
    Jersey City, NJ 07304; **201-433-7740**
IN CONNECTICUT
  202 Fairfield Ave., Bridgeport, CT 06604; **203-335-9913**
IN OHIO
  2105 Ontario St. (at Prospect Ave.), Cleveland, OH 44115; **216-621-9427**
  25 E. Eighth Street, Cincinnati, OH 45202; **513-721-4838**
IN PENNSYLVANIA
  1719 Chestnut Street, Philadelphia, PA 19103; **215-568-2638**
IN FLORIDA
  2700 Biscayne Blvd., Miami, FL 33137; **305-573-1618**
IN LOUISIANA
  4403 Veterans Memorial Blvd., Metairie, LA 70002; **504-887-7631;**
    504-887-0113
  1800 South Acadian Thruway, P.O. Box 2028, Baton Rouge, LA 70821
    504-343-4057; 504-343-3814
IN MISSOURI
  1001 Pine Street (at North 10th), St. Louis, MO 63101; **314-621-0346;**
    314-231-5522
IN ILLINOIS
  172 North Michigan Ave., Chicago, IL 60601; **312-346-4228**
IN TEXAS
  114 Main Plaza, San Antonio, TX 78205; **512-224-8101**
IN CALIFORNIA
  1570 Fifth Avenue, San Diego, CA 92101; **714-232-1442**
  46 Geary Street, San Francisco, CA 94108; **415-781-5180**
IN HAWAII
  1143 Bishop Street, Honolulu, HI 96813; **808-521-2731**
IN ALASKA
  750 West 5th Avenue, Anchorage AK 99501; **907-272-8183**
IN CANADA
  3022 Dufferin Street, Toronto 395, Ontario, Canada
IN ENGLAND
  57, Kensington Church Street, London W. 8, England
IN AUSTRALIA
  58 Abbotsford Rd., Homebush, N.S.W., Sydney 2140, Australia